PRAISE FOR ~~W...~~
ABOUT THIS ~~(...DAY)~~

"This memoir is exactly what we need: a hilarious, heartwarming book that reminds us that life, with all its ups and downs, is still beautiful."

—**BUNMI LADITAN**, bestselling author of *Confessions of a Domestic Failure* and humorist behind The Honest Toddler

"Anna Lind Thomas will make you laugh and cry and remember what it's like to get the giggles. Her stories are full of humor and heart and remind you that you can laugh about some of the worst times in your life . . . eventually."

—**CINDY CHUPACK**, *New York Times* bestselling author and Emmy-winning writer/producer of *Sex and the City, Modern Family, Otherhood*, and more

"Oh my gosh, I couldn't put this down. Anna's spectacular writing paints such a beautifully vivid picture that I felt like I was right there alongside her in these memories. I was laughing and nodding the whole time and couldn't devour it quickly enough. This memoir reminded me that while life isn't always perfect, we somehow always end up exactly where we are meant to be."

—**TIFFANY JENKINS**, bestselling author of *High Achiever* and humorist behind Juggling the Jenkins

"When I first met Anna Lind Thomas, she was better at everything than me (social media, writing, being funny), but she didn't act that way. She was kind and thoughtful, and I loved her instantly. So, if you only care about this book being hilarious and relatable, then guess what? You're in luck. But if you (like me) want the writer to be someone you'd split a bowl of queso with? Then you couldn't have made a better choice."

—**MELISSA RADKE**, author of *Eat Cake. Be Brave.* and star of USA's reality show *The Radkes*

"I knew I loved Anna's writing when I read about the fart that was heard (and smelled) around the world. But Anna is more than just a fartiste—her writing sparkles with honesty, insight, and warmth. If you're hungry for deep, bowel-loosening laughs along with a side dish of humanity and understanding, then get yourself a copy of this book. (And maybe pick up an air freshener too.)"

—**JOHANNA STEIN**, author of *How Not to Calm a Child on a Plane* and award-winning television writer and producer

WE'LL LAUGH ABOUT THIS

someday

WE'LL LAUGH ABOUT THIS

someday

ESSAYS ON TAKING LIFE
A *smidge* TOO SERIOUSLY

ANNA LIND THOMAS

NELSON
BOOKS

An Imprint of Thomas Nelson

Published in Nashville, Tennessee, by Nelson Books, an imprint of Thomas Nelson. Nelson Books and Thomas Nelson are registered trademarks of HarperCollins Christian Publishing, Inc.

Thomas Nelson titles may be purchased in bulk for educational, business, fundraising, or sales promotional use. For information, please email SpecialMarkets@ThomasNelson.com.

Unless otherwise noted, Scripture quotations are taken from *The Holy Bible: International Standard Version*. Release 2.0, Build 2015.02.09. Copyright © 1995-2014 by ISV Foundation. ALL RIGHTS RESERVED INTERNATIONALLY. Used by permission of Davidson Press, LLC.

Any internet addresses, phone numbers, or company or product information printed in this book are offered as a resource and are not intended in any way to be or to imply an endorsement by Thomas Nelson, nor does Thomas Nelson vouch for the existence, content, or services of these sites, phone numbers, companies, or products beyond the life of this book.

ISBN 978-1-4002-2197-4 (eBook)
ISBN 978-1-4002-2196-7 (TP)

Library of Congress Cataloging-in-Publication Data

Names: Thomas, Anna Lind, author.
Title: We'll laugh about this (someday) : essays on taking life a smidge too seriously / Anna Lind Thomas.
Description: Nashville, Tennessee : Thomas Nelson, [2021] | Includes bibliographical references. | Summary: "From popular humor writer and social media sensation Anna Lind Thomas comes an essay collection that is sure to make you laugh, cry, and cry from laughing as you discover how to take life a smidge less seriously"-- Provided by publisher.
Identifiers: LCCN 2021007006 (print) | LCCN 2021007007 (ebook) | ISBN 9781400221967 (paperback) | ISBN 9781400221974 (epub)
Subjects: LCSH: Conduct of life--Humor.
Classification: LCC PN6231.C6142 W46 2021 (print) | LCC PN6231.C6142 (ebook) | DDC 818/.602--dc23
LC record available at https://lccn.loc.gov/2021007006
LC ebook record available at https://lccn.loc.gov/2021007007

Printed in the United States of America

21 22 23 24 25 LSC 10 9 8 7 6 5 4 3 2 1

To my darling daughters, Lucy and Poppy—
the most hilarious little women I know.

CONTENTS

A LITTLE NOTE

Rob and I were sitting outside a breakfast café, sharing a gigantic cinnamon roll, when I asked how he'd feel if I stopped working a full-time job to pursue writing. I still remember the way he casually gave me his blessing as if my idea weren't an enormous, if not catastrophic, financial risk. He had left the air force and was a full-time nursing student. I mean, honestly, *what* was he thinking? But that's the way he's always been: a partner who moves completely out of the way so I can try my hardest to become the woman I'd like to be.

I immediately got to work on a website I called HaHas for HooHas. My best friend, Jen, and I (you'll notice Jen makes a lot of guest appearances in this book) created as much funny content for women as we could handle. I tried to post one funny essay per week, but I had a hard time coming up with material. I wasn't a good enough writer to make something interesting out of the mundane, so I needed outrageous stories to see me through the early years—and didn't have a whole lot of outrageous experiences to share.

It all changed one night when my parents had Rob and me over for dinner. Somehow the conversation led me to recapping a funny story of when I had farted on one of our first dates. We all laughed and laughed, but eventually I needed to wrap things up and get home. I took one last bite of mostaccioli and said, "Well, we better skedaddle. I have an essay I need to publish tomorrow on HooHas, and I have no idea what I'm going to write about."

Head tilted, my mom said, "Um, how about the story you just told us?"

I had a late start the next morning and needed to get to a dentist appointment, but I'd made a commitment to post an essay every Thursday morning, so I wasn't letting myself off the hook. In about thirty minutes I wrote an essay titled "The Fart That (Almost) Altered My Destiny." We had very few followers at the time, so I thought maybe a handful of friends and family members would slap a Like on it and that would be that. I couldn't have imagined that a new friend I'd met at a conference, a popular influencer, would read my essay and share it with her large audience. By the time I got home, my website had crashed.

I must say, I'm constantly tempted to rewrite the fart story. To make it better, funnier, more well written—with fewer exclamation points. But it's so loved, just as it is, that I think it's best not to touch it. I share the story again in this book for all the fart story lovers. You know who you are!

Really, when you think about it, the fart story is just some old-school potty humor. But it's more than that for me. I guess it's about a fart that didn't *almost* alter my destiny; it, in fact, altered my destiny *real good*. It helped me become a writer. And it also bailed Rob out of one of the worst financial decisions of his life.

Enjoy!
Anna

ONE

SPRING FRESH

Mom had missed her period, and there was
only one person to blame: Aunt Cathy.

Aunt Cathy denies culpability, of course. It's not
her fault Mom can't read a box. But I suppose
it doesn't really matter now. I'm here, and
there's no putting that cat back in the bag.

My story began in a freshly constructed home on an ordinary afternoon. Well, it *was* ordinary, right before the wallpaper man swung from the chandelier. My mother, Christine Lind, had two children at the time. Jenny was at kindergarten, and Christian had just finished nursing. Mom was walking him around the living room, gently thumping his back while his eyes grew heavy. She couldn't stop eyeing the burly wallpaper man working atop a makeshift scaffold in the entryway.

In those days, my father, Dick Lind, was just hitting his stride as a home builder. This meant building a home, moving his young family in before it was finished, selling it quickly, then moving them into another before Mom had time to file divorce papers. She was raising her babies surrounded by dust, strange men splattered in paint, the shrilling sound of table saws, and wall-quivering thumps during nap time. For a young mother of two trying to build a nest, it was a stone-cold nightmare. Not that she wanted an *actual divorce*, per se; she loved my dad. But she did fantasize about it every now and then while stain treating the bright-yellow baby poop on her new white capris.

This home was their biggest, grandest abode yet, with a cute little turret to the north side and a tall, bright entryway where the new architectural designer was working through a color swatch. The house reeked of sharp, sickly sweet lacquer, and my mom, crunchy far before her time, suspected the fumes were cancerous. Or poisonous. Best case, everyone was going to get fatty tumors. Regardless, she wasn't taking any chances. She opened the windows, but the day was warm. Her furniture, the same furniture she had just dusted a few hours before, was covered in yet another thin layer of dust. My brother spit up into the crease of her neck, and it dribbled slowly into her cleavage. Sweat speckled her upper lip.

The house typically bubbled with activity, but not on that particular afternoon. It was eerily quiet as she eyed the wallpaper man. From her vantage point, she could only see parts of the scaffolding and his big white Reeboks scuttling about freely like he wasn't high in the air on a wobbly piece of plywood. She laid my brother in his bassinet and was wiping her neck with a blanket when she saw the man's foot slip and the scaffold begin to collapse underneath him. She started toward him just as he grabbed the chandelier, his Reeboks swinging wildly. The designer was beneath him, clutching her swatches as the chandelier gave way. He dropped like an anvil, right on top of the designer. The wallpaper man grunted. The designer's back snapped. Mom screamed. And right then she made a decision. Christine Lind was done having children.

Over tuna casserole one night, Mom announced she was getting her tubes tied. It went over like a lead balloon. Dad sat across from her at the table, chewing slowly before saying gently, "Please don't; it's too rash." My dad would have had thirty kids if he could have gotten away with it, and I have to admit, he's a pretty great father. He's a doter—loving, attentive, and fun, and he can't for the life of him say no. Of course, this was back in the day of traditional gender roles, when dads weren't expected to participate in the day-to-day grind of parenting. Fatherhood's pretty easy if you've never dragged your limp, lifeless body out of bed to feed a screaming baby at three o'clock in the morning. Or suffered the indignities of a short-order cook while tiny idiots complain their grilled cheese is "too brown." The man didn't even discipline much; he just gave us whatever we wanted. The poor woman had enough on her plate. She was busy making tuna casseroles for tiny people who snubbed tuna casseroles.

Still, she respected his wishes and decided to take a pause on invasive surgeries. Getting her tubes tied was permanent and, frankly, sounded a smidge barbaric—like a doctor casually suggesting he make a square knot out of your intestines. Perhaps there was an alternative that sounded less terrifying. She decided on spermicide, an over-the-counter product guaranteed to go on a murderous sperm rampage on the user's behalf.

Mom may have known she was done having children the day the wallpaper man broke the designer's back, but she didn't know that in less than two years, she'd endure long hospital stays and endless nights rocking my sweet-natured, curly-haired brother as she sat on top of the toilet. Christian had contracted whooping cough. The shower would run hot, Mom's hair frizzing up from the sweltering steam. She would hum gently, her body no longer her own, given as comfort to a wheezing little boy. The agonizing wait to hear him take a breath after every cough dampened the joy of motherhood. The uncertainty of it all left little room for much else. Eventually, though, he got better. And the day she knew he'd be fine, her first thought wasn't *Let's have another baby!* It was *I think I'll start a book club!*

As her twenties came to a close and her two children grew older, Mom leaned in hard to her growing independence. She was feeling quite pleased with herself. She was fit, her skin was taut, her hair full, and her possibilities endless. My dad's home-building business was growing, and while they still moved a lot, it became easier with older children. She took pride in homemaking, enjoyed volunteering, and started to quilt with a bunch of old ladies because the world was her oyster. She worked diligently to prevent me, obviously, because her social life was in full bloom. Who wants to start over from scratch when you've just started sleeping through the night and your stitchwork is finally on point?

Then, sometime after Christmas, Aunt Cathy called. "Oh, Chris, you're not gonna believe this," she said breathlessly into the receiver. "There's a brand of spermicide that comes in disposable applicators now!"

Mom took in a sharp breath. "No!"

"Yes!" Aunt Cathy went on, painting a wondrous future in which neither woman had to store her applicators next to the toothpaste anymore. "Just put it right in the trash. Outta sight, outta mind!"

Mom leaned against the wall, full of wonder. Disposable applicators! What was next, phones without cords? This was the '80s, so things were bleak—women had to take aspirin for period cramps because ibuprofen wasn't available over the counter yet. They wore high-waisted, camel-toe jeans and sported bangs like tsunami tidal waves. Any progress for women and our feminine products was a giant leap for womankind.

Mom hung up the phone and looked at her Christmas tree, still festive but now dry and drooping. A few ornaments were holding on for dear life, while two had given up, released their grip, and landed on the tree skirt, hoping for the best. The tree, which had just a few days ago filled the whole house with holiday delight, was now nothing more than an inconvenient fire hazard. *New Year's Eve is in a few days*, she thought. *The perfect*

opportunity to buy the new spermicide and take it out for a spin.
She made her way down to the storage room, lugging up empty
Christmas boxes. Jenny and Christian were lying on their stomachs in front of the TV. Dad was dozing in and out on the couch.
Mom began carefully wrapping each ornament and putting it
away before losing steam. Her heart wasn't in it, and she needed
a quick distraction. She remembered she was out of coffee and a
few other pantry staples. She grabbed her keys, hopped into her
Buick Regal, and headed across town to the grocery store.

Sometimes I wonder, *Does the young stock boy who was tasked*
with organizing all the douches realize he played a key role in my
existence? And the butterfly effect this has caused? Just yesterday
I stopped a poor woman to let her know she had a surprisingly
long train of toilet paper stuck to her shoe, and you should have
seen her relief. I saved her from an entire day of humiliation.
Can you imagine her lot had I not existed? Thankfully for her,
decades prior, a stock boy displayed douches on the shelf just so,
unwittingly drawing the eye of Christine Lind.

My mom pulled up next to him, her cart bearing a can of
Folgers, a jar of cinnamon, and some moisturizer she didn't really
need but had grabbed anyway, thinking, *Oh, what the hell.* She
smiled at the stock boy as he took a step back to give her some
space. He fidgeted and looked up toward the ceiling because
watching a woman peruse feminine products made him feel all
uncomfortable, like walking in on your grandma shaving her

armpits. He decided to take his fifteen-minute break early. Mom scanned a package, blocking out key words like *douche* or *spring fresh*, and zeroed in on *disposable applicators* in order to complete her mission. She grabbed that puppy off the shelf and tossed it in the cart, where it bounced off the can of Folgers.

Armed with a fresh box of "contraceptives" and a new zest for life, my mom ran home into the arms of my father. I can see it now: Mom scuttling off into the bathroom, box in hand, to prepare for their tête-à-tête. I envision her beaming with the confidence that she was in control of her destiny. Her period had just ended, so she knew she wasn't ovulating, but she wanted to use protection anyway. One can never be too careful, amirite? And, if you recall the burly wallpaper man swinging from the chandelier, she'd made up her mind about future children. So, with the confidence of a village idiot, Mom took methodical measures to prevent me by douching herself right up while ovulating early.

Years later, as a teen, I asked her if the "fresh scent" while applying her "spermicide" had given her any pause, since that would be an odd thing to add to a spermicide. She told me she couldn't really remember.

"But didn't you see the word *douche* on the box?" I asked in distress.

"Apparently not," she said, wiping down the counter with a dish towel.

"So, I exist because you spring-fresh douched yourself on New Year's Eve before doing it with Dad? Oh, this is just . . ." I trailed off before getting up from the table. Although I was a teenager and old enough to know my parents had had sex at my conception, the fact that she'd douched beforehand added a layer I wasn't willing to accept.

Several days passed, and Mom's anxiety began to build when something wasn't right. Had it been over a week? She had lost count now. Every few hours she'd run to the bathroom, thinking maybe she had finally felt a little something down there. But nothing. Her period never came.

Mom didn't deserve this. She had done her due diligence. She'd purchased the spermicide. You know, the new kind of spermicide that had the word *douche* on the box and smelled like freshly washed sheets dried in the springtime sun. She had done her part. *Now providence, do yours!*

But it was too late. I was happening.

And Mom was devastated.

She cried a lot and spent two weeks in bed. My dad wasn't feeling particularly compassionate. The weeping just went on and on, and he had stuff to do. In his defense, a baby was on its way, not the bubonic plague. But in her defense, a human life is kind of a big deal. In fact, the introduction of a baby to any family is life altering for everyone involved. That babe requires an immense amount of selflessness on everyone's part just to keep it alive. And sometimes after years and years of selflessness, a woman just wants to think about herself and enjoy her life, on her terms. Even if just for little moments as her children grow older and she fears their deaths less when they play in another room.

The loneliness and dread swallowed her whole. Like a game of Chutes and Ladders, she had made her way through and started to believe she'd soon get a win. Then she'd rolled the dice, one last time, and landed on the big, obnoxious slide that shoots you all the way down, back to square one.

She put Jenny and Christian to bed and crawled into her own. Mom felt the small round curve of her belly. Somewhere I was in there, being knitted together by this and that. My DNA doled out orders, making sure I had my grandpa Gustav's long, thin Swedish nose and my mom's Sicilian brown eyes. My DNA also ordered a metabolism that's sleepy and smacks its lips a lot, like an old, fat bulldog. I also lack pinky toenails, so there was probably some room for improvement in the process. But, whatever, the job's done now, so it's best we move on.

It was then, as my DNA knitted together weird pinky toes, that my mom felt something else besides doom. It took her by surprise, although it wasn't surprising.

Love. All-encompassing, will-totally-kill-somebody-if-I-have-to love.

"It'll be a girl, and I'll call her Anna," she whispered to herself. (Oh, so Mom can't tell the difference between contraceptives and a douche, but she can get spot-on premonitions? I see how she rolls.)

But there, lonely in bed, she started to fall in love with me. Maybe being pregnant wasn't so serious. Yes, it again felt like the worst thing that could have happened to her. But maybe I could be the best thing to happen to her too.

She got herself out of bed and found my dad in the kitchen.

"We'll name her Anna," she told him as she wrapped her arms around his waist. "But no more moving our children into unfinished homes. And no more wallpaper men swinging from our chandeliers."

He agreed.

I don't know what happened to the wallpaper man, but the new designer fully recovered from her broken back. And that weird accident was one of the first steps to my existence. The fall that broke the designer's back was the straw that broke the camel's back, so to speak—the catalyst to my mom's spermicidal campaign against me. I'm sure that brings the designer little solace, as her back probably hurts like hell right before it rains. Of course, if Aunt Cathy hadn't recommended a spermicide Mom swears didn't exist (that Aunt Cathy insists *does* exist while claiming Mom needs to take responsibility for her own contraceptives) and the stock boy hadn't intermingled spermicide and douches to lead her off the scent, well, you'd probably be enjoying some other book from some other author. Frankly, I get jealous just thinking about it.

I've read that the chances of me being me or you being you are one in four hundred quadrillion.[1] It's a wonder any of us are even here at all.

I'm like a rare ruby in a gigantic pile of billions of rubies. Okay, fine. People are everywhere, and that can be real annoying, especially in traffic and while Christmas shopping. I guess with so many people milling about, none of us are really "special" per se. But at the same time, the odds we beat are too good for us to not have a precious, inherent worth. Even me, with my two freak

toes. And a laugh that's so loud it scares people and then gradually annoys them.

If my haters got a problem with it, they can take it up with
Aunt Cathy.

TWO

CHUBBY KIDS LAUGH LAST AND EAT FIRST

Mom was, and still is, a bit of a health freak—a real drag for a kid growing up in the '80s. During a time when dietitians were recommending a cup of Frosted Flakes each morning as a low-fat breakfast, Mom was grinding her own grain and churning butter like an Amish woman. She also replaced sugar with honey and bought plain, flavorless cereal that made you feel sad. In a world filled with Lucky Charms, my suffering knew no bounds.

Thankfully, I didn't suffer alone. My dad came to my rescue, often acting as my inside accomplice. Like a prisoner passing out small shampoo bottles filled with moonshine when the guard's back was turned, Dad was known to slip a little handful of chocolate chips into the modest bowl of raisins Mom had given me as a snack. Or give me a glass of chocolate milk made with leftover chocolate syrup Mom had used for ice cream sundaes at my brother's birthday party. I'd be reading *A Bargain for Frances* on the stairs when he'd hand me a glass. Afraid of the warden, I'd whisper, "Where's Mom?" with my eyes shifting side to side.

"She's in her room," he'd say, also whispering. "Stop worrying so much. I'm the dad, and I'm the boss." We both knew that wasn't true, but I'd believe anything for a tall glass of chocolate milk.

One time Mom offered to buy me an ice cream sandwich as a special treat from a local health-food grocery called No Name Nutrition. It should have been called "Nothing in Here Tastes Great If We're Being Honest." The store was operated by a staff wearing completely useless aluminum-free deodorant long before it was in fashion. I was hopeful when I picked out the treat from the freezer section, but it didn't take long for truth to reveal itself. A clerk with pit stains the size of serving platters invited us to her open lane, and after Mom paid, I slipped off the wrapper and gave it a try. Disappointment slapped me in the face. The cookie part of the ice cream sandwich tasted like cardboard, and the carob chips posing as chocolate chips offended me gravely. I still remember the look on Mom's face when I wouldn't finish it. Understanding, but a little put out. "It's all right; just throw it away," she said, waving me off. You can lead a horse to water, but you can't make it drink.

What Mom failed to predict was how I would behave once I

stepped out from her watchful eye. Like an Amish kid embarking on a Rumspringa ripper, I hit the hard suburban streets looking for any neon-colored freeze pops I could get my hands on. The trick was to select the houses where the parents were always out of sight but kept stockpiles of junk food for their kids and kids' friends to have without needing permission. Boxes of Capri Sun stacked against the walls. Every variety of Little Debbie cakes, Pop-Tarts, and Fruit Roll-Ups in the cupboards. And a car-sized variety pack of potato chips. I don't remember the name of the girl whose house I would party at, but I do remember my cheeks flushed from sweat on a muggy July day after polishing off my third Little Debbie Oatmeal Creme Pie in her garage. Like a secret smoker spraying down with Febreze before walking back into the house, I brushed off crumbs from my shirt and checked my face for frosting before hopping on my bike as the streetlights buzzed and flickered on.

I should have known Mom was up to no good when she called me down for fresh donuts. Pastries were reserved for the most special of occasions, and even then, my dad was the one who decided to buy them and bring them home. Mom would sigh, hands on her hips, feigning displeasure as if Dad had just brought home an English mastiff.

How could I have not picked up on her tone? She was far too casual and pleased with herself. I was reading a Little Critter book in my wooden rocking chair when she hollered the news. Mom might as well have said Santa was downstairs, I was so jazzed. I threw my book across the room and ran down the stairs, gripping the railing hard, taking two steps at a time, slipping and bouncing my butt off one or two. I finally emerged into a near-empty kitchen, huffing, looking around like a cop chasing a thief who had just slipped into the shadows.

"Yum, yum, yum!" Mom said, emerging from the darkness. "Whole grain donuts with a little honey drizzle. Have one!" She waved her arm like Vanna White, revealing a plate piled high with dark-brown mounds, shaped less like conventional donuts and more like the result of a child's craft project.

My sister was standing to the side, eating one of the donuts heartily. "They're not bad," she said. Her voice was stuffed, like she had a hot pad stuck in her throat. Maybe I was being too sensitive, but I was pretty sure there was an extreme injustice unfolding before my eyes and everyone was acting normal about it. The Bible says, "What father among you, if his son asks for bread, would give him a stone, or if he asks for a fish, would give him a snake instead of the fish?" (Luke 11:11). But I would go further and say, "What mother would tell her child there were donuts, only to serve her honey-glazed insults?" Not a good one; I was sure of that much.

Jenny continued to chomp away, like she was actually enjoying herself, and I was disgusted. I relied on her, as my older sister, my ally, to speak up for the children. Of all people, she knew this wasn't a donut. It was a mockery. And by the way—if these donuts were so delicious, where was my dad? Where was my brother? Somewhere in the house, not giving two craps about ancient-grain, honey-dipped donuts, that's where.

After a long silence, I spoke. "But why are they so dark brown?"

"Because," Mom said, picking up the plate, "I made them with fresh-ground whole grains. I fried them in olive oil and then drizzled honey all over them. This is what real donuts are supposed to look like, not that fake junk at the store. They are so good and so good for you, sweetheart. Go on." She pushed the plate toward me. "Try one."

These are what real donuts are supposed to look like? I thought. I might as well have been chatting with Tom Cruise as he defended Scientology. *I mean, do you even hear yourself?*

But I picked one up, sniffed it, and took a bite. At that point, it was simple charity for a mother who had just gone through an immense amount of work to treat her children with healthful foods. I chewed slowly. It wasn't gross, but it definitely wasn't anything close to a donut. It was the kind of thing people eat on the first week of their diet to try and convince themselves they're really gonna do it this time. "I don't feel deprived at all!" they say—the first clue they're either in denial or a liar.

Since her donut betrayal, a few decades have passed, and Mom's steely resolve for perfect health hasn't wavered. Her prairie-raised eggs taste like a piña colada gone wrong thanks to the huge dollop of unrefined coconut oil she sautés them in. But she's also softened her crunchy edges, enjoying foods of all kinds in their proper time and place.

Not too long ago, we were on our way to Whole Foods. I'd come to realize she wasn't a total health freak; she just had *freak tendencies.*

"Oh, I knew your father was slipping you treats," she said casually. "All I wanted to do was build you a strong foundation."

Mom rustled in her purse and opened up a piece of Wrigley's Juicy Fruit gum. "That way, if the house ever fell when you were an adult, you'd have something sturdy to rebuild on."

"Doesn't that have sugar in it?" I pointed out. As an adult, I began to adopt some of her health-freak tendencies and grew concerned the master no longer practiced what she preached.

"I'd rather have a little real sugar than that aspartame poison," she said, slipping it in her mouth. "And the gum you get at health stores tastes like flavorless rubber." I quietly agreed, recalling a time I burned through a twelve-dollar pack of health-food gum trying to chase that first hint of cinnamon before it slipped away like a wisp of smoke. Mom handed me a stick.

"This Juicy Fruit really is juicy," I said, almost disturbed by the amount of saliva collecting in my cheeks. Mom nodded in agreement. We both sat back and enjoyed a little sugar, smacking and smacking, all the way to Whole Foods to buy our eight-dollar prairie-raised eggs and coconut oil.

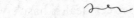

I could see my sixteen-year-old sister, sunbathing, glistening, shimmering, sparkling in the sun. Where she got the tanning oil and why she lathered herself in it, I couldn't tell you. She was at my swim lesson, not a Sandals resort.

"Oh, forget it," my mom said, rooting around in her purse. "The sun's too bright." On the way there, my sister had sat on Mom's sunglasses, breaking off the right arm. Mom eventually found what was left of her silver-rimmed shades, put them on, and looked toward the pool with dignity, as if she didn't have a pair of busted sunglasses on her face.

My swim instructors were blond, bronzed, eighteen-year-old twin boys, and it didn't take long to figure out why my sister had hopped in the car with us. The twins taught swim lessons in their parents' backyard pool on Tuesdays and Thursdays. I assume they were certified lifeguards and swim instructors, but it was the '80s, so who really knows.

They are responsible for one of two vivid moments in my life when my biology first awakened in the presence of handsomeness. The first seedling of my budding femininity breaking through the soil was when one took my hand and helped me into the pool. I felt something within me stir, like when an old bulldog lifts his drowsy head. The second awakening was a year or two later when I was at a friend's house after school. Her mom had left VH1 on while doing laundry. George Michael's "Faith" music video played, and, frankly, it changed me. As he shook his butt and danced on-screen, something within me stirred, and that drowsy bulldog turned into a full-on marching band, complete with a high-stepping drum major.

Back at the pool, the twins told me and my wispy classmates with superior metabolisms to hold on to the edge of the pool and practice our kicking. I flapped my legs furiously, eager to impress, splashing water up to my face, up my nose, and down my throat, causing me to puke out spats of chlorine water.

You wouldn't know it by the strength of my paddles, but I was feeling disappointed. My Mickey Mouse bathing suit left a lot to be desired. It clung to my meatier parts, and I protested as much, but no one in my family took me seriously. To them, I was their adorable "baby" in a Mickey Mouse swimsuit, and *fluffy, fluffy, fluffy* to boot!

Despite Mom's efforts to feed us only the very best, I've always been at various stages of "fluffy" my whole life. It's part genetic, part me being always down for a real good time. I don't know what being truly thin feels like. I imagine it's chilly and your bones are all knobby and vulnerable. I came close once, for about two weeks, in my early thirties. It was the thinnest I had ever been, and I recall my shock when I could no longer sleep on my side because of how much I hated feeling my knee bones rub. I bragged about it to my mom the following morning (who else can you truly brag to about weight loss?). "It's the craziest thing!" I shouted into the receiver. "I have to sleep with a pillow in between my legs now!" Then I laughed and laughed while peeling the shell off a hard-boiled egg.

As a child, though, it's very difficult to tell your family you feel a little self-conscious because when you're the baby of the family, everyone looks at you like they want to put you in between two hoagie buns and gobble you up. I was a person, for heaven's sake! With thoughts and ideas! Passions and pain! *Stop pinching my buns!* But they saw me as perfect, just as I was. And I was perfect. I was a healthy-sized little girl whom they loved. It's strange, though, how I felt so imperfect, so inadequate, *so fat.* Where did I learn it, and why did I accept it? I guess my innocence was simply chipped away by the outside world, a death-by-a-thousand-paper-cuts sort of thing. And it was just the beginning.

That day at the pool, I practiced my kicks on a paddleboard, with disciplined form and stamina. I kept glancing at the twins, sure they were impressed, but soon discovered neither of them was giving my stride a passing glance. They were too busy checking out my sister. She had a freshness, a sensuality about her I hadn't noticed before. I couldn't place what was making the difference. Maybe it was the way she was shaking her hair, the slight purse of her lips, or the way she dumped half a bottle of tanning oil all over her legs and then looked around aimlessly for a towel after she'd gone too far. The signals were sent, and the signals were strong. How could a fluffy child compete with that?

As young girls, we often had a delightful optimism that perhaps, while screaming and crying and singing our hearts out as NSYNC performed onstage, maybe, somehow, Justin Timberlake would come down offstage, see us, and instantly fall in love. What we'd do with that love, we had no idea, because we still had to be in bed by nine. Then we'd see those photos of him with Britney Spears and think, *I really gotta do something about these braces.*

And so it was with my clingy Mickey Mouse swimsuit—it just wasn't cutting the mustard.

These were the very first moments I became aware of beauty and feared it. I was locked between my family's constant praise and adoration and my own inkling of doubt that perhaps they were a little biased. It didn't help that my fresh new Dorothy Hamill haircut at a JCPenney hair salon was extremely disappointing. The stylist cut my hair behind the ear, making it more of a "If Dorothy Hamill were an eleven-year-old boy" haircut. Really, does anyone escape childhood unscathed?

I made my way across the pool on a red kickboard. Jenny glistened, her eyes closed against the sun. Mom smiled at me and waved, her broken sunglasses tilted to the side. So proud and so dignified.

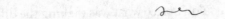

Taylor and I were bouncing about in her backyard, as third graders do, when we stopped to nibble on the cherry tomatoes growing in her family's small garden. She sighed and said, "My dad says I shouldn't eat too much or I'll get fat like you," casually, as if she were informing me one out of eleven adults suffers from type 2 diabetes.

Taylor lived on my street but didn't go to my elementary school, and I'm not even sure how we started playing together. My limited memory of her cuts like a ten-second movie preview, showcasing just the highlights. That particular highlight paved the road toward the dysfunctional Whitney and Bobby–esque love affair I now have with refined sugar. I still had a cherry tomato in my hand that I was just about to pop into my mouth when she whopped me with that comment. *What am I supposed to do with this tomato now?* I wondered.

I didn't have a lot of experience with sociopaths like Taylor, but a couple of years earlier (when I was quite normal sized, thank you very much), another little girl had thrown me similar shade. We lived right outside town in a beautiful country neighborhood. Although I don't recall specifics, I do remember Tia had black hair and she called me fat in her front yard. It wasn't to be mean, I don't think; she was just stating facts. Her name was spelled t-i-a, and I was standing in her yard f-a-t. It was the kind of insult little kids say plainly, observationally, usually after they've been staring at an adult for a little while. "How come,"—*Oh crap*—"you have such a huge"—*here we go*— "butt?" they ask, usually when we're feeling really good in the new high-rise leggings we confidently wore without a sweatshirt tied around our waist.

Regardless of Tia's intent, it was the first time anyone had ever insulted me, and I was aghast. I mean, I wasn't waify or lanky, and Mom never had to beg me to finish my lasagna. But I wasn't fat, and I knew it. My neighbor, Danielle, bore witness to the whole exchange and grew anxious under the tension. She was a year or two younger than me—a blonde, wispy little thing. She wanted to go home, so we walked back to her house quietly, both watching our step as we took the shortcut. I was chafed raw from the burrs but also from the false accusation. This couldn't stand. I had to clap back at my haters. So, with sweet little innocent Danielle in tow, I marched right back to Tia's house.

"Okay, so when we go up there," I said while Danielle and I high-stepped our way through tall grass, "pull on the back of my sweatshirt, nice and tight, so she can see I'm not fat." The plan was solid enough, and Danielle nodded in agreement, though we both sensed that being on my defense team was a bit out of her age range. But she was better than nothing, so we marched forward, renegades for justice. Tia was still in her front yard as we approached.

"Just so you know," I said, putting my hands on my hips, "I'm not fat. I'm just wearing a loose shirt." I lifted my arms, my cue for Danielle to pull the back of my white Esprit sweatshirt as hard as she could, but she just stood there, blowing on a dandelion. I shot her several eye darts until she finally remembered her cue and pulled hard on the back of my sweatshirt. I sucked in my gut and tried to say "See?" to emphasize my point, but I mostly mouthed it because I didn't have enough air in my lungs to get the word out. Tia just shrugged, then picked up her scooter and tried to make a go of it in the bumpy grass of her ill-kempt front yard.

Danielle and I turned back down the road to her house. I hadn't felt any satisfaction after our little demonstration, but what else could I do? Other than go back with a scale and weigh myself on her front stoop—which wasn't that bad of an idea, come to think of it. Eventually, I got bored and went home in time for dinner.

A few years later, out of the country and back in the city, Taylor's insult was made of a different substance than Tia's. It was darker, deeper, truer. At that time, I had actually become a fat kid. Well, *chubby* is a better word. I won't deny it: I liked to sneak into the kitchen when no one was around and dunk potato chips into ketchup. But I wasn't completely unhinged.

I was just old enough to be aware of my chubbiness and somehow knew that, at least according to the world I lived in, I should be ashamed of it. When Taylor affirmed what I feared was true, it was another paper cut—sharp, subtle, stinging, and far worse than it looked.

But the injury wasn't so much that Taylor, a child, had said this to me—it was that her dad, a grown-up, had said it *to her*. Using me (me!) as an example of something disgusting and to be avoided. *Wanna be a fatty like Anna?* I envisioned him asking a tiny Taylor, who then rigorously shook her head no. *Then stop asking for seconds.* Lava ran through my entire body, tingling up my neck, my chin, my ears. It was itchy, and I scratched at it like it was a rash. I don't remember what I did next. Did I go home? Act like it didn't happen and munch on more cherry tomatoes? Based on past experience, I can only assume I choked back tears and made up some excuse to go so I could let them out into my pillow.

Taylor's dad was a substitute teacher who stayed at home, and I don't remember what her mom did for a living. I only saw her a few times, and she was nice enough but not very warm. Her dad had a big, joyful, fun personality, but I detected a tinge of darkness in him. It was just a shadow, and I noticed it only because it was absent in my own father. For one reason or another—maybe it was the casual insults—I stopped hanging out with Taylor. Then one day I heard her dad's voice. He was substituting at my school and peeked in to say hello. "Anna Banana! You look good, kid!" he said with a wide smile. I really wanted to like him. I did. He was fun. And I wanted to believe he meant the compliment. But who was I kidding? I was just as chubby as ever. I stood there and waved back, my hand low, by my hip. In his defense, I bet he would have been horrified to know Taylor told me what he said. I couldn't help it, though. I hated him.

For the most part, I grew up in a family known to be fit and good-looking, a real drag for a late bloomer coming up behind the pack. Sure, it's fair to say that by now each of my family members has gone through a phase where they played it fast and loose with processed carbs, but really, who hasn't?

There was my dad, a strong, fit Swede. And my mom, a stunning Sicilian woman (for us Sicilians, we can really go one of two ways: Sophia Loren or Big Mama Mia with a mustache). My brother, Christian, was a buff star athlete, and my sister, Jenny, was pretty much all anyone could ever talk about. I was lucky though; she adored me. Jenny doted on and cared for me as if I were her very own, and her love made her beauty something I grew up admiring rather than resenting. I was acutely aware of how the world interacted with her beauty. Children sense those vibes, and I found that most people don't know what to do with themselves around a beautiful person. Others, though, just did what they wanted. Cars packed with young men would follow us around, honking and hollering. At the mall, some people would stop to tell us all how beautiful she was as if it were their duty as good citizens to inform us. Some stared—dumbfounded, mute. Boys would slip her notes and smile. Girls looked up, starry eyed. Others, particularly middle-aged women, glared.

In elementary school, there was a special day where our parents were invited to have lunch with us. My parents couldn't make it, so Jenny left work at the Estée Lauder counter early to come in their place. All the boys who knew of her got giddy and high-fived as if Candace Cameron from *Full House* were doing a meet and greet. One boy I had a huge crush on asked if he could come hang at my house after school. I delightfully agreed, until I realized it was a joke to get closer to my sister. *Like she'd be into some idiot who peed his pants last year*, I thought as my sweaty thighs streaked down the slide. *Give me a break!*

Does this kind of nonsense still happen to beautiful people, or have we finally gotten ahold of ourselves? I bet it still happens, just more subtly, since we're all supposed to pretend we don't care about physical beauty anymore. At least while writing our captions on Instagram.

It wasn't the people fumbling all over themselves that bothered me as much as the fact that they weren't fumbling all over themselves because of *me*. Were they blind? I wasn't just the baby in my family—I was the baby by a lot. My siblings were much older and at ages where they had the emotional freedom to adore, protect, and coddle me rather than try to smother me in my sleep. My adorableness was declared, like a guard announcing the queen, every time I sauntered into the family room. Where in the world was my applause? Where were my honks, my secret notes? And more satisfying, my glares?

I'm not proud of it, but one day I got so bored I decided to throw Taylor a bone and invite her over to play. It had been months since I had cut her out of my life, and I figured I would do a bit of charity in the afternoon. I extended the invitation, then noticed a cavalier tone in her voice as she expressed that she didn't really want to play with me anymore. "Oh yeah?" I said directly into the receiver. "Bite me." I hung up and found my parents watching me. I had learned the phrase *bite me* from *The Simpsons*, a show I wasn't allowed to watch. I clinched my butt cheeks as I waited for a reaction.

"Our little Annie," my mom said with a laugh. "A force to be reckoned with, I guess!"

Darn right, suckas. Something tingled within me. I wouldn't be made to feel invisible. Not by little girls, not by mean dads. Not by people who couldn't see past my sister's huge brown eyes. Not by the ladies who ever so gently suggested my mom grow my hair out and put me in more dresses, lest I become Rosie O'Donnell. Not by the vicious bullies I would later encounter in middle school or the men I loved in college who couldn't even remember my name.

This chubby girl would laugh last. I'd make sure of it.

But when would that be, exactly? I know this is a little depressing, but there are times I wonder if, at the end of my life, I will regret all the time I wasted hating my large, dimpled thighs, or if I will regret not knowing what life was like with thin ones. I hope I won't be thinking about my thighs at all, but with me you never know.

I'm almost forty now, and the chubby girl is still here. I hear it's your sixties when you really don't give a roaring rip about what other people think, but that seems so far away. The chubby girl seems to be frozen in time, a duplicate who never grew up. She's clipped my heels every step, every year. She doesn't always make herself known. She doesn't intrude. She takes vacations sometimes, or maybe stays in the lower level, out of my hair. But every once in a while, when my husband takes photos of precious moments between me and the girls and I later delete them with a "please tell me this isn't what I look like from the back"; or when my thighs swish together just so; or when someone ignores me, discards me, or tosses me aside—I feel her presence.

Through salty tears and a snotty nose, I look around for her hiding somewhere.

And I can usually spot her, peeking out behind a tree, a door, underneath my bed. She hides, but only because she wants to be found.

So I find her. I speak to her. I soothe her. *Oh no, no, no*, I assure her. *You aren't my shame; you are my most precious gift.* Without her, I surely would have focused on superficial things that appear beautiful one day but are thrown into the fire the next. I wouldn't have, instead, spent hundreds of hours reading and writing in my room. If beauty had been my hot ticket, I wouldn't have made laughter into a craft. I would have become colder, less compassionate, more flippant, and crueler if I didn't know the pain she endured. Her pain made me more whole.

So, I thank her, and this usually makes her feel better. Then I look away for just a moment—maybe I get a text or the timer on the oven goes off. And before I know it, she's gone, skipping away, still wearing her white Esprit sweatshirt, nice and loose. Just the way she likes it.

Bite me, Tia.

THREE

MY PERIOD, MERLE, AND ME

What's Jenny doing on the floor?" I asked.

I had sauntered into my parents' room looking for my markers. Mom was at her bathroom counter, close to the mirror, mouth agape, applying mascara. My sister was behind her, lying on the ground. I could only see her legs, and one foot was moving, methodically, swishing back and forth.

"I explained to her how tampons work and—*boom*—down she went," Mom said, putting the cap back on her mascara and slipping it into a drawer.

"Oh," I said as my sister's foot continued pacing. "Do you know where my markers are?"

Jenny faints easily, usually at the sight of, thought of, or mere mention of blood. Under normal circumstances, watching someone faint is a fairly dramatic affair, one that includes lots of nervous energy as people shout loudly, slap faces, and ask one another if a call to 911 is in order. But we had all gotten pretty used to Jenny fainting by then, so as long as she hadn't hit her head on her way down, or knocked a serving tray of hot coffee all over herself, we would just wait for her to rouse and go back to business as usual.

I'm no fainter, though. Hit me with the cold hard facts of womanhood and I'll make it work. When it was my time to step over the threshold of my feminine mystique, I vowed to take the realities of tampon wearing head-on. Some girls think the start of their period is the worst day of their lives, but I welcomed the opportunity. I've always been eager for the next thing, the next step, the next big moment of my life, so much so that I rarely appreciate the life I'm currently living. I admired my sister with such tenacity. I was leaping toward my time to shine, to bleed through my bedsheets, to take more Advil than advised on the bottle, to force the nearest man to shop a bullet-pointed list of treats, tampons, and pads. I was ready to lie in the fetal position for two days just like all the other brave women of the world.

It should really have been no surprise that, out of all the days of my life for my period to come a-calling, it would choose the day I was away from the safety of my family and on vacation with my best friend and her father.

Merle was a blue-collar, burly, gruff but kind man. He was a carpenter and close to my dad, the two of them often working together on my dad's houses. Lacy and I were the same age and became fast friends, growing up together, spending the night, and practically living at each other's houses. Although, obviously, we preferred her house because Merle was a single dad who let us do whatever we wanted and bought us everything we asked for.

It was summer, and he was helping to build a series of fast-food restaurants in Memphis, Tennessee. He took us with him for a small vacation, to do a little sightseeing. While packing, I questioned how many pairs of underwear I should bring. We were going to be gone for no more than four days, so one would naturally think four pairs was sufficient. But since I was eleven, showers weren't really something I'd choose willingly on any given day. I'd be having lunch in the kitchen when my mom would tilt her head and narrow her eyes. "When was the last time you took a bath?" she'd ask. I'd stare back, blink a few times, then take a bite out of an apple. "You're taking one tonight," she'd say over her shoulder, while exiting the kitchen.

I've always been one to put my best foot forward, preferably when other people are watching, so the underwear debate brewed in my mind. I knew a courtesy "I'm hopping in the shower because this is what people are supposed to do after a long, hot day in the muggy Memphis sun—right? Or is it cool if I just sit here and relax? Okay, no, I'll hop in the shower," would likely be expected. Maybe even a few. My mom had just bought me a twelve pack of white cotton briefs, triple the amount I needed. Perhaps it was some inner knowing, the intervention of a guardian angel, or I just couldn't be bothered to open a pack of underwear, but I threw the entire pack in my bag and zipped that puppy up.

We were staying at a Holiday Inn when it happened. Merle was on his bed, reading a newspaper. Lacy and I were on ours, lying on our stomachs, watching *Full House*. I didn't notice anything amiss and eventually got up to use the bathroom. As I sat, what I witnessed before me terrified me to my core. I had crapped my pants.

I took off my underwear, bundled the evidence up, and slipped it into my pocket. I pulled up my shorts and then, ever so casually, waltzed into the main room, pretending to look for something in my suitcase. Then I shoved my underwear in a secret pouch. Why I didn't just throw the underwear away, I can't tell you, but it's probably because eleven-year-olds are gross. I took out a fresh pair of briefs, which I again slipped subtly into my pocket before moseying back into the bathroom to put those on with nobody the wiser.

This went on all four days, and I was tearing through my twelve pack of undies at a breakneck speed. There's a picture of Lacy and me outside of Elvis Presley's mansion, and although you wouldn't notice, I can see the turmoil tossing away in my insides like a down pillow in a dryer. *I'm pooping my pants*, my eyes confess. *And yet, I feel no sensation of pooping.* My heart wails, *Every time I go to the bathroom, it's like opening a present from the devil!* My stomach is lurching. *And the look of it! It's not normal! It's weird! Ominous! Death! In Memphis! With Merle!*

On the last day of our trip, I was in my last pair of underwear, and my pleadings with God were really ramping up. I wore the burden of my secret like a soaked wool shawl. Obviously, opening up to Merle about my grim prognosis and the eleven pairs of poopy underwear shoved into the side pocket of my suitcase was out of the question. And I couldn't tell Lacy because she'd just tell him anyway. I vowed to confess my secret to my mom the minute I got home, but when I finally got home, I just couldn't bring myself to do it.

The whole day went by, and I had faked several pleasantries without sharing a peep of my harrowing experience.

"I saw Lisa Marie's favorite chair at the mansion," I told my family over dinner. "And a rip in the pool table some guy in Elvis's entourage made while attempting a pool trick. But honestly, all I really wanted to see was his bedroom and the bathroom he died in, but they wouldn't let us." The fact Elvis died on the toilet, pooping, was an irony not lost on me, I can assure you.

My choice to not disclose my dire secret was motivated by a mixture of embarrassment and fear that maybe something was actually wrong with me. The next evening, Mom asked me to take my dirty clothes from my suitcase and put them in the laundry room. I pulled my wrecked briefs out of the suitcase, gingerly, as if the folds of cloth were wrapped around the lifeless body of a baby squirrel that I was shamefully stowing away—like one of those creepy kids you really want to keep your eye on. I knew the minute she found these in the laundry, the jig was up. After a few deep breaths to muster my courage, I went to her room. She was sitting on her bed, reading a *Victoria* magazine, illuminated by the yellow hue of her lamp.

"Mom?" I said, making my way toward her.

"Yes?"

"I have something to tell you."

"All right," she said, setting the magazine on her lap.

"I, um . . . Well, I um . . ." I turned my gaze away. "I keep pooping my pants. I pooped the entire time I was in Memphis. But I don't feel like I have to poop, I just find out I pooped later when I go to the bathroom," I said. "And it looks like, well . . . it looks like I'm really, um, sick."

"Show me," Mom said. I left for my room and brought back the entire pile, dumping the briefs on her bed.

"See?"

"Oh, honey," Mom said, sitting back in her pillow. "That's not poop. You've started your period!"

"I did?" I said, with the same inflection people use when they find out they won the Publishers Clearing House sweepstakes. Then a grin coiled around my cheeks. "I did. I really, really did."

I long assumed the first day of my period would be met with some sort of parade or fanfare, balloons dropping, trumpets sounding, or, worst case, an ice cream cone with sprinkles. But the way my period began was pretty much on brand for me—an embarrassing tale to be kept to myself. Still, I thought it better to put my "continuously crapped pants under the care of Merle" mishap behind me and approach womanhood with pride.

This new budding femininity did something to me. My shoulders went back, my walk became a saunter, and my confidence blew out of my ears. I grabbed my sister's box of tampons to read the tiny leaflet inside. I was taking full responsibility for my womanly education, and by the time I was done, I'd dare you to quiz me on toxic shock syndrome!

I left to go study in my room and ran into my sister in the hallway. "What are you doing with my tampons?" she asked, her face turning pale. She steadied herself against the wall.

"I'm a woman now," I said with my head held high. *Pfffft. Amateur.*

"Oh, Anna?" Mom called out. "Get this pile of dirty underwear off my bed, please."

I stopped in the hallway and turned, holding the box of tampons like a coveted prize. *It would be my pleasure.*

FOUR

YOU'RE WELCOME, LADY GAGA

got on the bus really feeling myself. It was a hot day, windows were propped down, and kids lined the aisle with flushed, beaded, salty faces. I adjusted my large round glasses slipping from my nose and grinned wide. A few of my friends high-fived me; others laughed, gasping, unable to believe what was unfolding before them. It's rare to witness the sweet slap of justice with your own eyes, but when you do, it's very sweet indeed.

If you looked all the way through the back of the bus, you could see my older brother, Christian, a high school senior and muscular athlete, wagging his finger in Sam's face. His friend, a towering buff wrestler, stood by Christian with his arms crossed like a bodyguard. You couldn't hear what my brother was saying, but you could see his finger jutting out toward Sam. It was fascinating to see Sam so terrified; you could nearly see the currents of fear waving through his body. He even looked like he might cry. Oh, the delight! My friend Adrienne squealed and put out her hand for a low five. What a hot, muggy, vengeful day to be alive!

"Your brother's a douchebag!" some teenager in the back of the bus said to me as I sat down. That was a bit troublesome and unexpected, but the moment was too delicious to be spoiled by one rotten apple. "Sam's just a kid, man, that's messed up."

But Sam wasn't just a kid. He was the most sadistic person I have ever known. That's an uncomfortable thing to say about a middle schooler, but he was the kind of bully who would beat you down until you sobbed, then laugh as he stepped in your puddle of tears. Most of us have had our own experiences with a mean bully, but rarely of this kind. This was the kind ferocious enough to make headlines.

I'm not sure what made Sam set his eyes on me specifically, but I was chubby with a fresh new boyfriend, so that probably explains it. Alex and I announced our relationship formally to our friends. "We're together now," we'd say, holding hands on the bus. "Officially boyfriend and girlfriend." Then I'd go sit with my girlfriends, he'd move to sit with the boys, and we'd sort of forget that we were together. Alex was handsome, especially for the seventh grade. I don't know why, but going back to elementary school, he just adored me. He was my very first kiss, my first love. The first boy who made my heart pitter-patter. He looked like Aladdin, or an adolescent Tom Cruise, and I looked like Carnie Wilson with a short perm.

Sam was appalled by our arrangement, and in every class we had together, he would sit behind me and whisper the deadliest insults. "You are by far the fattest, ugliest person I've ever seen," he'd hiss. "Alex just feels sorry for you; trust me." Then he'd touch my curly hair in disgust. My shoulders would lurch toward my ears, my body slowly covering itself in sweat. I recall one time, after the teacher had called on me to answer a question and I got the answer wrong, he leaned in and said, "Fat, ugly, and really stupid. You are so gross." This went on day after day after day.

I never told my parents, and if I did, my version was so watered down there was really no flavor. I did this a bit for their own hearts, but mostly to temper my humiliation. But over the course of months, silence became deadlier than action. I gathered my courage and told my brother everything, begging him for help. "Sure," he said casually, cramming a huge spoonful of Cheerios into his mouth. "Where do you want me to meet you?" I'd hoped he'd be a touch more offended on my behalf, but beggars can't be choosers.

The next day's wall-to-wall manic energy hit a crescendo as the final school bell rang. I pushed through the heavy doors to see my brother standing there, smoking a cigarette. He flicked it away when he saw me and blew smoke from the side of his mouth. I was appalled to see him smoking and made a mental note to tattle on him later. "Where is he?" Christian asked. I looked around while kids oozed like lava from the school's doors. As the flow turned into a trickle, I got nervous. The buses were rattling, anxious to depart. Exhaust swirled around and choked us. I glared at the doors, trying my hand at telekinesis, luring Sam out with my own desperation to not lose this opportunity. It must have worked because, just like that, there he was.

"There," I said, pointing at Sam.

"That little nerd?" Christian said, as if he'd been expecting some large dopey bully, like Buzz McCallister, Kevin's older brother in *Home Alone*. I nodded. Christian signaled to his friend, and they walked toward Sam. I boarded the bus, redeemed.

After that day, Sam never spoke to me, looked at me, or even dared to come near me again. Neither did his sidekick, Matt, who had occasionally begged to be my boyfriend while pretending to be intellectually disabled. He'd profess his love while pounding his chest with the side of his hand and make grunting sounds like Chunk from *The Goonies*. But after my brother's confrontation, Matt's eyes shot to the ground and never looked up at me again. Those questioning the inherent sin of man need not look much further than middle school.

Sometimes I think about people who don't have someone to stand up and protect them. What do they do when the Sams of the world try to dismantle the DNA of their spirits? I'm not advocating vigilante justice (well, maybe I am), but there's something beautiful and poetic about a person who will step in and kick someone in the jewels for you.

About five years ago, I was commissioned by an online magazine to write a piece on bullying after the suicide of a sweet boy had made the news. I began my research and wondered if I should find Sam. Perhaps I'd make this into a riveting piece of confrontation and reconciliation, which would of course go viral, get me on the *TODAY* show, and win me a Pulitzer or something. I like to turn lemons into lemonade, know what I mean? I googled his name, and one lone picture appeared of a terrifying man. Same evil eyes. Same black hair, wild and unkempt. He was grinning, baring jagged, mustard-yellow teeth. It was his mug shot. The cruelest kid I had ever known had become a meth addict, rotting away in jail because he had stabbed someone to death in an alley.

Well then. I guess that explains it.

"Five, four, three, two, one," I whispered to myself. And after the *one*, I spoke out loud in my class for the first time. Like someone hyping herself up to jump out of a plane, I had to do a countdown to speak. I don't remember what I said, but I remember people laughed. It was the most beautiful sound. I was a freshman in high school, sitting in English class. I'd like to tell you things got better after a grim junior high experience. And they did, in a way. To their credit, high school kids were a lot nicer. It's like we all agreed to call a truce so we could focus on the hellish landscape of emerging adulthood. Similar, I suppose, to a couple fighting while driving in a car and promptly setting the disagreement aside when they get caught up in a thunderstorm. But the fear of being bullied, at least for me, was just replaced with something duller and blunter: FOMO. The popular acronym stands for *fear of missing out*, the nonlethal yet troubling electric voltage that rides through my body when people are audacious enough to enjoy one another's company without me.

"What's your problem?" Mom asked me while I sat with my parents in the living room, watching a rerun of *Seinfeld*.

"I don't have a problem," I snapped, arms crossed. "And can we watch something else? *Seinfeld* is stupid." Dad laughed at the intensity of my outburst, and Mom rolled her eyes, but no one entertained turning the channel.

I was lying, of course. I did have a problem. A big problem. It was a Friday night, and no one had called me to hang out. I was sitting there with my loving parents, well-fed, clothed, and warm, and it was more than I could possibly bear. This moment summed up most of my high school experience—the constant rummaging through the emotional wreckage of needing to be liked and included.

I suppose it's this way for a lot of people, but I've always been opposing threads of yarn, intertwined seamlessly to make one person. For example, in a "geez, get a grip" sort of way, I want everyone to like me, but I personally don't like people all that much. I mean, sure, I like them in a general sense, but in the moments of my life where other people are present, I can usually take them or leave them. I'm awed by warm, engaging people. Those who take the time to notice and honor others. You know the types—they ask every person who comes across their path questions *and actually care about the answers.* I've always wanted to be this way. I've asked God to help me be this way, and I've gotten better. But it's not my natural temperament, and most often, I can't be bothered. Unless, of course, you can do something for me—like give me something or help me advance in some way. Then I'll roll out the red carpet, pour the champagne, and, with consent, provide a gentle shoulder massage as we carry on delightful banter. I'm an introvert, not an idiot.

My opposing threads make other patterns too. I'm frightfully ambitious and will work on a goal until my body, brain, or close relationships collapse. Yet I'm also quite lazy and will defiantly refuse to leave the couch for hours on end as if my back has gone out. I come alive when I entertain, perform, and make people laugh, but I'm shy and dread it. I live for a fun girls' night, but when the time hits to put on a decent bra, update yesterday's makeup, and head out, I huff and puff, hem and haw, as if I'm putting on coveralls to start my shift as a gravedigger. I don't actually want to do the things other people are doing. I simply want to be invited so I can politely decline on my terms. Surely I'm not alone in this.

My mom had it easy. I would never, ever, bring negative attention to myself. This was, and still is, akin to death in my view. I know few enjoy getting embarrassed in public, but I take it especially poorly. And it's not just my own negative behavior that concerns me, but your behavior by proxy. If we're dear friends and you start making a scene, I'll walk away slowly and deny ever knowing you. When the cops show up, I'll give a false statement. I'll lie under oath; I don't care. If I'm the one who created the scene (I'd never make one intentionally; get serious), I'll deny it was me, and it'll be convincing. I don't care if you have video footage, that's my cousin Anana, and yes, she has an uncanny resemblance. Unless you got DNA evidence, I suggest we all move on.

So parenting me was a breeze. Not because I wasn't naughty—I was just as naughty as the next kid throwing a fit in aisle 5. But I would have rather died than have people witness me behaving naughty in public. Why would I want them staring at me and casting their judgments? Skittles aren't worth it, and I wouldn't give them the satisfaction. All of this was part of my constant—and ongoing—tug of war. It's difficult to reconcile my nature. I guess you could say if everything is just right—the goal, the person, the occasion—I'll go all in. And if it isn't just right, I'll melt away and dribble into the gutter.

Or, I suppose you could look at it another way.

I care deeply about what other people think. And I resent it.

All my friends enjoyed, and often swapped, boyfriends. I, on the other hand, had a serious fling with strawberry Pop-Tarts—a little treat I'd get myself at school every morning, slipping some quarters into the vending machine, just to help see me through. Over time, I made friends with a group of popular girls, and our friendships waxed and waned and evolved throughout high school. But I myself was never popular. Most of them were beautiful and thin or had that wholesome Katie Holmes look that made the boys go wild—while I was usually in the background as entertainment.

Fiesta was probably the most popular girl in our school. I

was jealous of how much she was liked and adored, but I mostly admired her. She was the class president, well-connected, and friendly with everyone, even the outcasts, nerds, goths, and theater geeks. One day, we went to the bathroom together. At the sink, she said, "Can I ask you a question?"

I shook the water off my hands and reached for a paper towel. "Of course."

"It's a little embarrassing," she said, turning off the tap. "But—do you think I'm popular?"

I stared back at her, then blinked a few times. "Uh, yeah."

The most popular girl in school was insecure about her popularity. Was there hope for any of us?

I was never officially asked to any homecomings or proms. I'd secure my plus-one by negotiating with guys who also didn't have dates and didn't really care that much. My senior year, I asked an old friend, Luke Carl, to go with me. I knew him from middle school. We'd been in band together; he played the drums. We shared a close mutual friend who suggested I ask Luke to be my date. He happily agreed, excited to go to another school's prom. He was extremely tall, six foot five, maybe. I remember dancing with him and resting my head on what felt like his stomach. There wasn't much romance sparked between us, but we had fun. After graduation, I went to the University of Nebraska–Lincoln, and he moved to Brooklyn.

Luke reinvented himself in New York, as they all do, I suppose, and wanted to be a rocker, emulating the '80s hair band look. He grew out his black hair and wore leather vests with no shirt underneath, tight black jeans, and black boots. His tall

frame became thin and lanky, like Tommy Lee. He was managing a bar in Lower Manhattan, and we'd chat every so often on
Myspace. One day he messaged me:

> I'm doing good. I'm having a hard time with my
> girlfriend, though—so things are kinda rough I guess.

I responded:

> Oh? She's your girlfriend now? That girl you've been
> talking about who comes into your bar a lot?

He replied:

> Yeah, I love her, but I can't see it working.

Luke, despite his look, was straitlaced, and while he was
in the scene, he didn't partake in the scene. Maybe it was that
Nebraska boy in him. His girlfriend, on the other hand, partied
a lot and dabbled in things he didn't approve of.

It was hard to imagine him in Brooklyn—managing a bar, no
less—rocking out and brushing up against the unsavory things
like drugs and sex and rock and roll.

> That's not you, Luke. Follow your gut and let her go. You
> deserve so much better. You'll find the right woman for
> you, in the right time.

I felt satisfied with myself, figuring this was how Oprah must feel when one of her guests had a breakthrough. I waited a few moments for his reply. I was like a counselor who sits quietly, allowing space for truth to bubble to the surface.

Yeah, you're right. Okay, gotta go open up the bar. Ttyl.

Luke and I talked casually, usually superficially, off and on until it eased into a slow drip that eventually stopped. Years later, after I lived in California, I married Rob and moved back to Omaha. One day I was on my couch, sleepily watching *E! News*, when the host said, "Lady Gaga has been seen with on-again, off-again boyfriend Luke Carl," except the caption at the bottom spelled his name Lüc Carl. I slipped into an alternate universe.

I sat up and stared at the TV screen, my brain rapidly attempting to process the images I was seeing. Lady Gaga, in a pool, on the back of the kid I went to prom with. I whipped out my phone and fell into a Google rabbit hole, the experience probably not far off from what Alice experienced.

I charted a timeline that, while imperfect, gave me an indisputable story line. After the Myspace chat with Luke, he broke up with his girlfriend, Stefani Germanotta, a young woman who had frequented Luke's—sorry, Lüc's—bar and fallen in love with him. After their breakup, she was left devastated but found the courage to transform her grief into art, writing songs called "Poker Face" and "Bad Romance." She called herself Lady Gaga, got a record deal, and became an international phenomenon.

According to *E!*, they were now back together, gallivanting in some swimming pool.

So, as you can see, I am 100 percent responsible for her incredible launch into stardom. If I had not encouraged Luke—sorry, Lüc—to dump her, they wouldn't have broken up, she wouldn't have been inspired to write chart-topping hits, and none of this would have ever happened. Lüc and Gaga wouldn't have eventually gotten back together, inspiring her to write songs like "Yoü and I" and continue her soaring global fame. In short, YOU'RE WELCOME, LADY GAGA. And quite frankly, YOU'RE WELCOME, WORLD.

Truth be told, I think Stefani (can I call her Stefani?) and I would be great friends. Better than Lüc and I had ever been, that's for sure. I see it so clearly: after a full day of relaxing in her mansion, squeezing our own fresh mango juice and laughing and laughing, she'd thank me deeply for my hand in her career. I'd smile, and she'd be comforted by the tenderness in my eyes. "I'm not responsible for all this," I'd say, waving my hand holding the cup of fresh mango juice around her palatial family room. "You are. It was your strength, your talent, your hard work, your despair that got you here. I just ... maybe ... I don't know," I'd say sheepishly, setting my glass down, "put a little gas in the tank." Then I'd pat her hand, and we'd sit in the joyful silence of our friendship.

At just the right moment, I'd speak again. "Did I ever tell you about the time I was bullied by a murderer?" She'd put her hand on her heart and encourage me to open mine. I'd share my harrowing tale. She'd have a few ruthless bully stories of her own, and we'd cry a little, then laugh a little too. Then she'd get on the piano and sing for me. "Know this one?" she'd ask.

"Oh, I don't know, Stef," I'd say with a mischievous grin. "'Shallow' is a little played out, don't you think?" After all, as my friend, she'd come to rely on my honesty. "Try another," I'd say.

She'd nod, pressing her fingers into the white keys, and sing "Telephone" as a ballad, just for us.

And we'd spend the whole day together, just like this. Because she'd really, really like me.

FIVE

WE'LL LAUGH ABOUT THIS . . . SOMEDAY

We had about thirty minutes of daylight left, and that's when my panic sank so deep it was swallowed by darker, more peaceful waters. Through labored breaths, I began to gently sing old church hymns. If you know me personally, then you also know that if I start singing old church hymns (in my loveliest vibrato, no less) and it's not a joke—I'm likely foreshadowing someone's untimely death. Probably mine.

We were surrounded by trees so massive, so ancient, I didn't feel like I was in nature; I felt like I was on a Universal Studios lot, shooting a scene in *Jurassic Park*. It had an otherworldly eeriness, as if a velociraptor might peek out from behind one of the huge trees, grinning, teeth bared. And I could barely see my hand in front of my face. We were so dead.

I was hiking with my best friend from college, Jen. I had just moved to Chico, California, and was working at California State University as a resident director while getting my master's degree. After I got settled, she flew out for a visit and already had our itinerary planned. Jen's the highly organized adventure type. You know the kind. They make agendas for your trip to Hawaii and find the most incredible deals on flights. Some people get annoyed when they feel like their vacation or "relaxing weekend" has been hijacked by this type, but I *adore them.*

What she really wanted to do more than anything else was hike in the redwood forest. I was thinking more along the lines of wine country, but whatever.

I should've paid attention to the fact that Jen hadn't done much research before the trip. It wasn't a long drive, but too long to make it there and back in a day, so we decided to wing it and book a Hilton or Marriott when we arrived in town. Worst case, a Holiday Inn. We were flexible.

Of course, if we had actually done our research, we would have known that wasn't happening—and probably would have packed some mace.

Our first mistake was that we had no proper understanding of what "hike in the redwoods" actually meant, and we'd made no effort to learn. We packed a meager overnight bag and wore sweatshirts with running shoes. Feeling smug and extra prepared, we also brought backpacks "just in case." Mine had a mint cookie

Balance Bar and a small bottled water in it. Jen's bag had hand sanitizer, Burger King napkins, a lemonade vitaminwater, and a gel pen.

The drive through the scenic mountains was glorious. We picked up road snacks and laughed and laughed. Looking back, this was our second omen. My memory is like the opening scene of a horror movie—a car full of teenage girls, laughing, gossiping, having fun. You just know what's going to happen. This isn't some dreadfully scripted feel-good movie, like Britney Spears's *Crossroads*. These fools are about to run out of gas on some rural road, stumble upon a dilapidated house, and eventually get chainsawed. And the idiots don't even see it coming!

As we rolled into town, we were quick to notice a strong meth-crisis vibe.

"Keep an eye out for a Marriott," I said, hanging on to a positive attitude as we passed our first functioning motel, which looked more like a run-down convenience store from the '60s. We kept driving, and a Marriott kept not appearing. *Not even a Super 8.*

"Let's just stay here," Jen said, pointing to yet another could-possibly-be-abandoned motel.

"Oh, Jen, this is a motel you book for an overdose. We can't."

"Who cares? It will make a great story," she said, her voice trailing off as we caught sight of a large, very hairy, shirtless man wearing shorty shorts and sitting on a plastic lawn chair outside his room.

Jen and I have always thrown ourselves willingly into weird situations. We do it simply for the story to tell later. Once, we signed up to be secret shoppers at Disney World, and another time, we jumped in the middle of a parade, pretending we were part of it. As a budding writer, I couldn't get enough of these types of experiences, so this run-down motel, while giving me pause, did have a kind of perverse appeal. *Worst-case scenario*, I told myself, *Jen gets murdered, and I escape within an inch of my life. That's easily a bestseller; I don't even have to try hard. Maybe it'll get optioned for a TV movie and I'll be played by Jennifer Lawrence.*

We walked into the motel office, which was more like a screened porch. I rang the call bell, and a woman (I like to call her Barb) emerged through a sliding glass door that appeared to lead into her apartment. And through the door I could see a huge, grizzly man (whom I'll call Gus) sitting in a dirty recliner and drinking a Bud. It was better than my wildest dreams.

She gave us keys to our room. I expected the worst, hoping for the best.

We went in and were relieved there wasn't a bloodstain on the carpet, but when I checked the shower, the door fell off the hinges as I held it by the handle. This place was so bad it was good. But we didn't have time to relish the moment much longer; we had a full day of hiking ahead of us, and we were losing daylight. I propped the shower door against the wall, dropped off our overnight bags, and locked up behind us.

"So, I grabbed a map," Jen said as we got into the car, "and I think we should do this trail right here."

I listened, satisfied. God bless controlling vacation planners.

"It's one big loop," she continued, "and according to this here, it should take about three hours. We'll finish with plenty of sunlight and time to clean up and go out to dinner."

"Woot woot!" I shouted, pumping my arm.

As we approached the start of the trail, we couldn't believe our eyes. The sun cast a yellow canvas on top of what looked like a Bob Ross painting. Except these weren't happy little trees. They were more like old, grumpy, gargantuan trees that held lots of unsavory secrets. According to the map, our trail would start off winding through what appeared to be an open prairie. Eventually the trail would lead us deep into the redwood forest.

The prairie part looked nice on paper, but it was pure nonsense. I tripped at every step, and it was soon obvious I needed more of a hiking boot that protected my ankle than a clearance pair of Nike sneakers. I wouldn't say I was worried, but I did start to feel vulnerable. This wasn't like the trails in Nebraska I was used to, where you could stop and sit on a bench to throw some Wonder Bread at geese. This required a certain level of skill and athleticism, of which I had neither. But I did have a Balance Bar.

"Is that an eagle circling above us?" I asked Jen, pointing toward the sky.

"Uh, no, that's a vulture," she said, descending into her deep laugh.

"Maybe there's something dead around here," I said nervously, looking to and fro. "Are there any bears or other wildlife we should be worried about?"

"Um, I think there are bears here, but I'm not worried. How many times do you hear of people being killed by bears in Redwood?"

Her response wasn't overly comforting, but I'm not much of a worrier by design. I kept walking, watching my steps carefully, until I felt a whoosh that forced me to stop abruptly. Jen bumped into my back.

"What? What's wrong?" she asked.

"Oh no," I said. "Oh no, no, no, no, no, no."

"What?"

"Did you pack tampons?"

"What?"

"Tampons. Do you have some?"

"Oh no. No, no. Maybe you peed," Jen encouraged me, as if that were a more acceptable and plausible option. I pulled out the elastic waist on my yoga pants and looked down. "Is it bad?" she asked.

I looked her square in the eyes. "It's bad."

She shuddered, flipped her backpack around, and grabbed the Burger King napkins. "Here. Shove these down there and let's go. We don't have a lot of sunlight left." Then she lathered her hands in Purell.

We walked quietly, enjoying the view and carefully watching our steps. My mind wandered every so often toward bears mauling and eating me. "So, um, what if bears are attracted to me now?"

"What? Oh stop. You'll be fine."

Again, not really all that comforting, but what choice did I have? We were about to enter the forest.

The first step was like entering a Harry Potter book. Dark magic was happening somewhere, probably near the herd of centaurs. Still, we made the most of it, taking time to snap candid pictures of ourselves near or inside some of the most captivating trees, laughing and giggling and unknowingly leaving a trail of photographic evidence in case we went missing.

I perked up, though, when we started to hear the chatter of other humans. Emerging from the depths, we saw hikers making their way toward us. They had huge packs on their backs, filled with all sorts of survival gear, like tents, axes, and fire kits. They wore mountain-climbing-grade hiking boots and used walking sticks to help navigate the terrain.

"Hello!" Jen said with enthusiasm. "How's the view down there?" But no one answered her, except for one guy who gave us a nod and a grunt. As each hiker passed, they looked us up and down like we were wearing hot-pink leotards.

"Rude," Jen said behind the back of her hand.

"Are you sure we're on the right trail?" I asked. "Why are they dressed like that?" We stopped and Jen pulled out the map.

"No, this is the one. We're fine," she said with a shrug, putting the brochure back in her pocket.

The initial part of the trail into the woods went down the mountain before swooping up and around back to the starting place. The skyscraper trees already made it dark and gloomy, but I could see the sun slowly descending through thin slivers. My ankles were caked in dirt and sweat, and I felt blisters forming where the back of my shoe rubbed. I winced right as a stark observation occurred to me.

"Hey Jen, it's been almost three hours, and we're still going downhill. If this is a loop, shouldn't we be going up by now?"

She stopped. "Has it really been three hours?"

"I think so. Didn't we start at four?"

She pulled out her map and scanned quickly, looking for something we might have missed.

"Oh no."

"What?"

"I read this wrong. I'm so sorry."

"What?"

"Oh my god, Anna—I'm so sorry."

"*What!*"

"This isn't a three-hour trail—it's a three-*day* trail."

We stared at each other. The redwoods paused; not a single leaf moved. Calm Anna was fleeing the scene, and end-is-nigh Anna was taking up residence.

"Maybe we can call the police or a forest ranger," she said, whipping out her phone. I grabbed mine too—no signal. In about an hour, we'd lose the sun, leaving us in a pitch-black prehistoric forest that dipped to freezing temperatures at night. It had taken us nearly three hours to make it down; now we only had one hour to make it *up.*

"We're gonna die," I said matter-of-factly. There was no use panicking. This was the end.

Jen grabbed me by the arms, her eyes growing wild. "Look," she said, "I'm not sure where we are on the map, but at some point it says we'll hit a rest area at the bottom. Someone may be there and can give us a ride up."

"What if no one's there? That doesn't help us at all!" I'd already begun to picture all kinds of harrowing deaths we might endure before our bodies were discovered—or at least whatever body parts were still left to be found. "This is so bad, Jen. This is *so* bad."

She shook me. "Look at me, Anna. *Look at me!* Then we have no choice but to go back up. We can do it, you hear me? We can do it." Her aggressive pep talk conjured something inside me, despite the spittle that flew out of her mouth and hit the corner of my eye. I flinched and gritted my teeth.

We could do this.

I mean, I think so?

If we didn't make it out of the forest before nightfall, we would have to spoon right there on the trail in a freezing, hostile climate as deadly wild animals encircled us. The girl on her period was gonna go first; that much was obvious. Although, if I can be completely transparent, I didn't fear death half as much as I feared an entire evening of enduring my period without a tampon or Advil to see me through.

Nah, I wasn't going out like that. It was time to make a run for it.

"Okay, okay," I said. "We can do this!" Then I pushed Jen aside and sprinted up the mountain, wild and determined.

Jen stayed close behind me, and we ran as fast as we could for as long as we could until our lungs burned. The sun was barely visible through the trees, the trail disappearing before our eyes. Through labored breaths, I pulled out my Balance Bar and rationed a portion for Jen. She shoveled it into her mouth like a starving little squirrel.

"I'm going to leave my Balance Bar wrapper here on the trail," I said, breathless. "My friends know this is my favorite flavor, so maybe it will help lead a trail to our bodies." That was an actual sentence I said out loud, with sincerity. But we'd clearly both crossed into a new, hysterical dimension because Jen, usually quick to find humor in outrageous situations, had the eyes of someone who had just been stuffed into the trunk of a car.

(Looking back now, though—*geeeeez*. Drama much?)

We started to settle into an eerie acceptance, and ever so quietly, Jen began to sing a church hymn. "Holy, Holy, Holy! Lord God Almighty . . ."

I joined her in chorus. "God in three persons, blessed Trinity . . ." We quietly walked a few more meters before I asked, "Jen? Can you sing that again?"

"Sure," she said with a sad smile, as if she were bedside at a hospice.

But she was interrupted by a terrifying sound. I grabbed her hand and shushed her. She stopped singing, and we circled around back to back, scanning the dark forest for the sound's origin. Through the rustle of leaves we heard it again—a low, guttural, nasty growl.

Have you ever noticed the phenomenon that if two people are drinking and one starts to get way too drunk, the other will often sober up to protect the drunk friend? The same is true of hysteria. I was equally terrified, but Jen's wild eyes told me that she was about to dive headfirst into the abyss, and we just didn't have the time. I had two options: slap her across the face or lie. Since I had never actually slapped someone across the face and the whole concept scared me a little (How much oomph do you put into it? And how far is too far?), I went with lying.

"Jen, calm down. *Calm down*." I grabbed her shoulders. "It was just a creaky tree. I promise!"

"Oh god! Are you sure?"

"Yes! It wasn't a bear. Relax. Just a creaky tree. Just a creaky tree. Deep breaths. There you go. Deep breaths, deep breaths. That's it." She took huge gulps of air, and as she quieted down, I shoved her aside and sprinted up the mountain like a Jackie Joyner-Kersee who'd really let herself go.

This was about survival now. Cold, hard, do-what-has-to-be-done survival. And since I was the one on my period, keeping her behind me was my only chance.

She was in fast pursuit after me, periodically hollering out, "I thought it was just a creaky tree!" This time there was no stopping to catch our breath. Like gazelles, we leaped over fallen branches the size of motor homes, and like ninjas, slid under them. Occasionally we'd both bellow out involuntary bursts of screams. With our backpacks whipping side to side and our boobs swinging in wide circular motions, untethered by nonathletic bras, we kept a pace only made possible by pure, unfiltered adrenaline.

"Look!" I screamed. "I see sunlight! We're almost out of the forest!" We sprinted now, at a pace far beyond our natural athletic abilities, until we burst out of the forest like twin baby girls from a birth canal.

Back on the prairie, we hunched over, hands on our knees, sort of cry laughing, sometimes dry heaving. We were probably going to live!

My feet were swollen and blistered, rising like warm loaves of bread spilling out of a pan, but I trudged through the prairie, tripping repeatedly on knots of long grass. We put one foot in front of the other until finally the car was in sight. The sun officially dipped below the horizon as I flopped into the driver's seat and slammed the door.

Now that we were alive and totally fine, the crazed panic of the last hour started to feel a bit awkward. We'd been completely out of our minds, and now we were back in the car as if nothing had happened. Flashbacks of our fretting and screaming about a forest like it was some kind of haunted house would swarm around our heads until we slapped them away.

Like, *Jen, remember when we screamed that we were going to die while holding each other? What a hoot!*

Or, *Hey, Anna, remember when you littered your Balance Bar wrapper on the trail so forest rangers would be able to identify our bodies? What a scream!*

"Looking at the size of that ankle blister, I'm sure you don't have much of a sense of humor," Jen said, breaking the silence. "But, we'll laugh about this . . . someday." She chuckled softly, trailing off as she looked out the window. I put the key into the ignition, and we drove in silence back to the motel.

"Hold On" by Wilson Phillips quietly played on the stereo, but neither of us felt festive enough to belt out our usual harmonies. We just hummed to ourselves, mouthing the lyrics. As we curved around a bend, the headlights drew something into focus. It was a cluster of people standing in the middle of the road. "What . . . what the . . . what's happening here?" I said out loud, forcefully pressing my foot on the brake.

They waved their arms and pointed at us, signaling for us to pull over. They didn't look official, as if they had the authority to pull us over. They were mostly women, model-like, but with dirty, bare feet and hairy armpits—very à la Charles Manson— except for two men leaning up against an old VW van on the side of the road. One man was smoking and had a sexy Patrick Swayze vibe, but in a leader-of-a-sex-cult sort of way. It's possible I watch too many Quentin Tarantino movies, but seriously, guys, you can't make this stuff up.

"What is this?" I asked again. "Do I pull over or what?" Jen let out her maniacal, albeit exhausted, laugh. I crept the car along the road and faced that I had only two choices: stop and pull over or hit the gas and trample these freaks. I wasn't confident enough to properly run a person over, let alone multiple persons, so I slowly came to a stop. About seven of them encircled us.

"Thank you so much," the one who appeared to be in charge said. She pressed her hand on my window. "Can you roll this down?"

"Nope!" I slipped my hand up and flicked the door lock button.

"Oh, okay, um, our battery died. Can you please help us jump it?"

Jen and I looked at each other again, trying to communicate our distress without being overtly offensive. When things like this happen in the beginning of scary movies, you're often in disbelief people are so stupid. *Just drive around them! Hit them with your car if you have to!* you think to yourself in disgust.

But when you watch a scary movie, you're already in on the secret that bad things are destined to happen. In real life, while experiencing something so out of the norm, your brain doesn't act fast; it's too busy rapidly scanning all the data it can process. Mix that with a little bit of shock and denial and a natural desire to people please, and you have a recipe for two young women pulling over on a dark, isolated road to become the newest members of a modern sex cult.

Jen and I stayed in the car and gave zero indications we were open to small talk. I checked my phone—still no service. *Blast this forsaken town.* Soon it became apparent they didn't want us in their sex cult (rude) and really did just need a jump. I popped the hood from the inside of the car and prayed they wouldn't steal the battery or the engine or jack us up and take our wheels because, honestly, I was exhausted and in no position to resist. My ankles had blisters. Just do what you gotta do, ya know?

After a few turns, they were able to start their van, and they waved us off with a thumbs-up. As I began to merge back onto the road, however, we heard their van shudder and go dead once again. "Wait, stop! Please, stop!" the women shouted in chorus. But there was no stopping this time. I hit the gas and spun gravel in their faces. Enough is enough!

We made it back to the motel, now hollowed-out versions of our once-cheerful selves. As we got out of the car, I checked my phone, and we finally had a glimmer of cell service. I pressed the button to see if I had missed any calls when the phone slipped through my hand, bouncing off the concrete. It shattered instantly as if it were glass. I looked down, admired the menagerie of pieces that had once made up my phone, stepped on it, and kept walking. Limping, dirty, and cold from sweat, we hobbled toward our motel room, and Jen fumbled for the keys. She turned the lock and kicked the door to our room wide open.

"Oh, hello," said a man in an Australian accent, lying in my bed.

YOU CAN'T BE SERIOUS.

"Can we help you?" said the other man, lying in Jen's bed.

"Uhhh . . . this is our room!" we shouted in a synchronized scream. At first glance, I'm sure Jen and I looked like we were on the tail end of a three-day meth bender.

"No, this is our room, I'm afraid," said the one in my bed. Why were they acting so casual?

"Those are our bags!" we shouted again.

"We wondered about those," said the other. "I don't know what to tell you, loves. You're welcome to sleep on the floor, but this is the room she gave us." My brain did a quick scan for potential dangers. The men weren't the least bit threatened by us. They were wearing tight spandex uniforms with logos on them, bikes propped up against the wall. They must have been on some bike-riding excursion, which helped me relax a bit and hesitantly scratch off "potential murderers" from my mental list.

"Yeah, I don't think so," I said, grabbing our bags. We stormed off, and I was sure to give them the Sicilian look of death as I started limping toward the office (front porch). I rang the office "doorbell" feverishly.

Out came Barb, nonchalant (the audacity!) and in a robe, with her hair in actual curlers. "Can I help you, girls?"

"Uh, yeah—you gave two guys keys to our room?"

"Oh, I did? Sorry about that," she said, shuffling to the board with dangling keys. What was the deal with these people acting as if this were normal? "That happens from time to time."

After a few seconds, Jenny and I smirked at each other, the fear and frustration melting away and our love for a good story reminding us we had a keeper. We felt satisfied. With the threat of death safely behind us, we could lower our shoulders from our ears.

While Barb retrieved our key, I waved at Gus, who appeared to have never moved from his recliner. He didn't return my pleasantry, so he was likely ignoring me. Or dead.

How do you even begin to tell an outsider what happened to us that day?

New key in hand, I turned to leave the porch, then stopped at the door. "Oh, Barb?"

"Yes, dear?" she asked from the other side of the screen.

"Do you know where I can get some tampons?"

SIX

WHADDYA HAVE TO LOSE?

———

Mom's text said it was all very, very sad, but Lucy was throwing up. The buzz of her text had woken me up, and when I first read the words, I froze, as if her text were a T. rex that couldn't find me if I stayed perfectly still. I had disabled my "read" receipt years ago, so I suppose, even though my mom's text did indeed find me, she couldn't prove it.

I scrunched my pillow under my head and rolled to my side. I tried to elbow my way mentally into a peaceful sleep, but now that I knew Lucy was ralphing at Mom's house, I couldn't unknow it—and what it meant for the rest of us. The week prior, my friend Danelle had texted me that her son, Auggie, who goes to the same preschool as my girls, Lucy and Poppy, had started projectile vomiting in his car seat on the way to school. As Danelle took a U-turn home, the school office sent out a medical notice of confirmed cases of a stomach virus. Oddly, I didn't get the same notice she did, so I allowed myself to believe that her experience was irrelevant to my life.

A few days later, Danelle texted me a follow-up as her husband was performing a puke/scream combo in the master bathroom. "It's so loud, Anna," she texted, terrified. "It's bad. Really bad." Then, an hour later, her daughter went down. And a mere three hours after that, Danelle tumbled down after her. "Now I'm puking up sips of water!" her text read, almost like a Morse code SOS—as her entire house sank, down, down, down, like a battleship.

Now, it was coming for me.

I patted my husband's shoulder as he groaned. "Mom just texted me," I said. "Lucy's throwing up."

"What?" he said, squinting at me harshly, as a vampire would seeing the morning sun peek through the blinds. Then he said, "No," firmly and rolled over to go back to sleep.

"Lucy has that stomach bug going around; we have to go get her, Rob," I said. "Come on. Let's go."

We were savoring our last gasps of a very rare freedom—like a brief conjugal visit at a state prison. My parents had offered to take the girls for two full days. The day before, Rob and I had eaten at a new restaurant in town called Timber. Maybe it was the freedom talking, but it was the best food we had ever eaten and best cocktails we had ever sipped. Then we'd giggled home and stayed up late watching movies, eating salty-sweet popcorn. We'd planned to sleep in, then go on a walk around a gorgeous park by the lake. Afterward, back to Timber for a delicious brunch with the bottomless mimosas our charismatic server had sold me on. "Is there some kind of fancy french toast?" I'd asked, trying to take a sip out of an empty glass. "Oh, sweetheart, you have no idea," she'd said, signaling she'd get me another. "Ask to sit in my section. I'll take care of you." After planning to have the best brunch of my life, and friending my server BFF on Facebook, I planned for Rob and me to relax until dinnertime, where we'd eat dinner with my parents and lazily make our way home with the girls.

As a parent, I've grown accustomed to disappointments in my personal life. The seats to *The Nutcracker* left empty because Lucy came down with a fever fifteen minutes before we were supposed to leave. The conference I couldn't attend because I was still nursing. The movie I had to leave fifteen minutes in with a gas-stricken baby screaming over my shoulder. The trip I had to cancel because the sitter fell through. Now I've learned to make plans that probably won't happen, simply because a girl must never stop dreaming.

Rob lay in bed, unable to come to grips with what I'd told him, while I put my foot through the wrong leg hole of my shorts and tried to get myself together just enough so that I wouldn't be horrified if we got in some kind of fender bender and had to actually get out of the car. Somehow, we pried ourselves out the door, picked up the girls, and got back home, where both of them took turns throwing up in a small bathroom trash can I had set by their makeshift beds on the couch. Poppy took us by surprise during one bout, catching me in the cleavage and our bulldog, Bruno, on his back leg. After they were done, they spent the rest of the day cuddling on the couch, drinking Sprite and nibbling on saltine crackers.

Rob and I sat with them, nibbling on our own sleeve of saltines—not despondent, but more pensive. Like people who had finally accepted their terminal diagnosis and made the decision to stop resisting and simply cherish the few remaining good days they had left. Five days later, it was Rob's turn to slip right down the toilet. And two days after that, I slithered my way down to the cool bathroom tile, where I rested my clammy cheek, cursing the anonymous child who'd stepped foot into our preschool and brought that poison to us all.

At around three in the morning, I was no longer vomiting, but I was still feverish and couldn't sleep. So I went to the couch and started watching a show on Netflix called *Love on the Spectrum*. I was looking for a show that was interesting, but not so interesting I couldn't say goodbye to it if sleep finally came calling. I had already watched *The Great British Bake Off* ad nauseam and craved something fresh.

Love on the Spectrum is a series about various adults on the autism spectrum pursuing romantic relationships. All of them faced challenges, from mental to physical to social. But what made them all so beautiful, so pure, so true was their inherent desire to love and be loved with their whole hearts. They recognized love as the key that unlocked their humanity, and little else seemed to matter.

One woman stuck out as my favorite. Her name was Maddi, and she had Asperger's syndrome, a form of autism that affects the ability to effectively socialize and communicate. She had never been in a romantic relationship before and sometimes told the truth so flat out it was both jarring and incredibly gratifying. Before a potential blind date, Maddi was asked what she was looking for in a romantic partner. She said, bluntly, she wanted a man who was "rich, muscular, tall." When her parents burst out laughing, she proclaimed, "There's no shame in being picky when it comes to love."[2]

Oh, how I could relate to Maddi. We were two women who knew exactly what we wanted and didn't see any reason to compromise. Even in high school, when I was wearing Gap men's sweater vests, I knew I was deserving of the very best.

Oh yes. We'd get everything we wanted, Maddi and me—eventually. Probably. Maybe. Oh please, Lord. *Please.*

Rob and I met on Match.com back when it wasn't cool for people to marry strangers they'd met on the internet. Now it's almost embarrassing if you didn't meet your new partner online. "You met him at a party?" your coworker might say at happy hour, cocktail in hand. "Like, a Facebook Watch Party, or . . . ?" But back when Rob and I decided to log on to find love, it wasn't a thing. It wasn't publicly shunned, but most people privately judged it. Meeting someone online implied that potential suitors had seen you in person and decided "Eh, rather not." So the only place for you to turn before your eggs hard-boiled was the one place nerds, men with hairy shoulders, and predators felt free to socialize and be themselves.

Yet, there I was, creating my account for a two-week free trial. I was driven, in part, by Dr. Phil's encouragement. At the time, he was the spokesman for Match.com, and I don't totally remember the tagline, but they were promoting the trial, and he said something like, "Whaddya have to lose?" in his trustworthy, down-home drawl. I mean, if Oprah's right-hand man thought I had nothing to lose, maybe I had nothing to lose. Besides, I was simply window-shopping. I didn't expect to find anything I'd want to take home, but I was open to being pleasantly surprised.

Mere moments after filling out my exhaustive questionnaire, I had to find the perfect photo to upload. This was no easy task, as we were all still on flip phones at the time and didn't have five thousand pictures of ourselves in our pockets. I landed on some distant black-and-white photo of me looking in the mirror as I put on lipstick. It was one of those "behind the scenes" wedding photos when I was a bridesmaid at my friend's wedding and probably not ideal for a dating profile photo, but how was I supposed to know?

I have to admit, I wasn't overly impressed my first go-around. My criteria generated scant results—students I couldn't date because of my position at CSU or skinny men who couldn't grow mustaches but were trying very, *very* hard. Every once in a while I'd get an email from Match letting me know someone had winked at me, and most of those were from men in their sixties. Their pictures would be blurred, the lighting would be horrendous, and it appeared all of them were in some type of camper trailer. They'd say something like, "I know I'm out of your preferred age range, but you're real gorgeous, and I'd love to buy you a beer."

After a while, I decided Dr. Phil hadn't been quite right; I did have a little bit to lose. I stopped logging on and forgot about it until I got the email informing me it was the last day of my trial and providing a list of my latest Matches. The very top one was a man named Rob Thomas. He looked cute and normal and worked at an air force base about an hour away. On a whim, I logged on and messaged him:

> Hi there!
>
> I'm really bad at this whole Match thing. I did the two-week free trial, and it's my last day—I'm not signing up. I think you're cute and pretty normal looking! Here's my email address and you can just email me directly if you're interested—anna_lind_81@yahoo.com.
>
> Hope to hear from you!
>
> Anna

After about an hour, I got an email from an address that had the word *matchbox* in the title. I groaned. Was that a reference to Matchbox Twenty because of his name, Rob Thomas? Okay, fine, whatever.

> Hi!
>
> I can't believe I caught the attention of a beautiful woman like you! I'm not good with this Match stuff either. Can I take you to dinner and we get to know each other a little better there?
>
> Let me know what you think.
>
> Rob

Hey, hey!

Luckily you were surrounded by 60+-year-old men wearing bandannas and living in camper trailers, so you stuck out so nicely! How does this Friday at 7 sound? Olive Garden right by the mall, off the hwy in Chico?

Anna

Wassup!

Sounds perfect. See you then!

Rob

The "wassup" gave me great pause, and I now feared I'd rushed way too fast into dinner. I'm not that superficial, truly, but a big negative to online dating is there's no physical or social cues to help guide attraction and compatibility. Chatting with a man you have great chemistry with allows an occasional (preferably just one) "wassup" to slide in without dramatic effect. But online, all you're left with is a two-dimensional profile picture, grammar, and the misguided use of commas to determine your future. For one Match named Mike, I spent an entire hour trying to figure out if his jeans were actually hoisted up past his belly button as a style choice or if it was a mirage because of how he was crouched. *Do I risk winking back? WHY DID I SIGN UP FOR THIS?*

But that's where I met my husband. This is the first time I've openly admitted meeting Rob this way. The vast majority of my longtime friends and acquaintances reading this right now are thinking, *What the heck, man? You said some friends at church set you up!* or *Wait, wait, wait, wait, wait. Hold up. So Rob wasn't the good Samaritan who pulled you out of your burning car when you crashed on the highway? Wait. WAS THERE EVEN A CRASH AT ALL?*

The times have changed, and I'm now proud to finally say it: I met my husband online. I guess I didn't have anything to lose.

For our first date, I arrived early at the Olive Garden. I tried really hard not to, but there wasn't any traffic, and all the lights were green. It was very annoying. I sat in the car and peered into the entryway. I saw a very tall man looking at his phone. Check! He looked muscular too. Check! Check! Now, about the rich part . . .

To this day I'm not completely sure what I was thinking with the outfit I wore. I have an inherent desire to be feminine and beautiful, but my desire to be comfortable overrides it entirely. Which means if I have to choose between a tight pair of pencil pants to wear on a date or an oversized pair of basketball shorts, I'll probably go with shorts and hope my big, curly hair sees me through. What I chose wasn't bad, I suppose, but I could have done better. I wore black stretchy pants from New York & Company that were basically yoga pants passing for professional attire. And then, curiously, I wore a black polo shirt. It was an ensemble your hungover cousin would throw together for Grandma's funeral.

After Rob and I sealed the date earlier that week, not a single carb had passed my lips. I'd hoped to drop about fifteen pounds in a couple days. I have to admit, I was feeling a little slimmer as I opened the door to the restaurant. Rob and I recognized each other, smiled politely, and shook hands. I don't know how to explain it, other than to say when I saw him, I saw my husband.

I never felt this way looking at any other man. It was as if I had always known who my husband would be. And then—there he was. Everything I imagined.

As we sat down, I could tell Rob was having a love-at-first-sight moment too. I've had men attracted to me, lust after me, barely notice me, be completely turned off by me, but this was the first time I saw with my very own eyes a man falling head over heels for me. I could tell he was nervous because he was talking at a rapid pace, where there were no gaps or breaths in between his words. It wasn't a turnoff; it was endearing. I listened patiently while purposefully posing in several flattering positions.

It was all so exciting that I decided to eat whatever I wanted and enjoy our time together. Which, if you've been eating virtually zero carbs, is a very bad idea. I didn't want to be "that girl" so I ate, drank, and, oh, was I merry.

After dinner, we decided to shop a bit at the nearby mall. Rob drove us over in his Mustang Cobra, and his pathetic attempt to win me over with a car totally worked. I'm not shallow, but since I spent most of my twenties picking men up in my car because I didn't want my hair to frizz in their un-air-conditioned jalopies on three wheels and a fifteen-year-old spare, I welcomed his fancy sports car with open arms.

As we shopped, Rob surprised me by buying an expensive pair of shoes that he caught me eyeing. Was this love?

That's when it happened. Gas strikes in two different ways—uncontrollable toots or sharp, shooting pains that feel a lot like dying. I thought I was dying. Not to make a scene, I told Rob I suddenly wasn't feeling well and probably needed to head home.

The pain was so intense I asked for a ride. I'd have my coworker help me pick up my car later.

On our way back to my apartment in his Cobra, he tried to hold my hand and ask me lots of questions, but I wasn't having any of it. The pain was so bad it felt like I was being stabbed with a bunch of tiny forks. Then I realized . . .

My God, help me. I have a horrendous fart on deck. I'm in trouble. Big trouble.

The more I held it in, the more pain would shoot through my stomach and down my legs. I was even having to raise myself off the seat, gripping on to my door and the dashboard.

"Seriously, you need to hurry—I'm in a lot of pain," I managed to say through gritted teeth.

"Wow, it's that bad? What's wrong? Do I need to take you to a hospital?"

How do you tell a man you just started dating that the reason you're writhing in pain is because you have to fart?

Well, you can either tell him, or, like me, let the fart speak for itself.

People, hear me. There was nothing I could do. As impressive as I am with sphincter control, this was out of my hands. Slowly, it eked out. The more I tried to stop it, the more it forced its way through the door. However, to my pleasant surprise, there was no sound. I sat silently, sweat accumulating above my upper lip. *Okay, maybe I got away with it. Maybe I'm home-free.* Then it hit me. Not an idea—a cloud. A horrific fart cloud. Not in an "Am I smelling something?" sort of way. More like an "Is someone dead and rotting in your trunk, and am I in hell?" sort of way.

Suddenly, I panicked. "Roll down the windows!" I screamed. (Yes, I literally screamed it like I was in a horror movie.)

"What? Why?" Rob asked, starting to freak out because I was freaking out.

"I can't roll down the windows. Unlock it! Unlock it!"

"What's going on?" Rob yelled back to me. "Why are you . . ." Then it hit him. I could see it in his eyes. Was it surprise? Horror? Water started to accumulate at the base of his eyelids. "Oh my god, I can *taste it*!" he screamed.

"Roll down the windows!" As I screamed, the toots started to flood out uncontrollably. I scratched and clawed at the window like I was being kidnapped. Rob, unable to see either by fart cloud or panic, kept turning on the windshield wipers instead of unlocking the windows.

It was chaos. We were acting like we were under siege by gunfire. We were under siege, all right, just not by gunfire.

Finally, he was able to hit the right control and rolled down our windows. We both gulped in fresh air. I was horrified yet happy to be alive. Then I remembered I'd just farted on the man of my dreams, and I sorta wished I were dead.

We sat in silence for the rest of the way home. Although the shooting pains had subsided, I now desperately needed to use the bathroom, in an urgent, explosive kind of way.

He pulled up to my apartment, and before he could come to a stop, I had already jumped out. "Okay, thanks for dinner, sorry about the fart, love the shoes!" I shouted and ran into my apartment like I was running from the cops.

I burst through my door and ran straight for the bathroom,

where I was finally able to unleash and make noises that no one should ever, *ever* hear coming from another person.

Then I heard Rob's voice. Right. Outside. My. Bathroom. Door.

"Anna? You left your shoes in my car, and your front door was open. Where do you want me to put them?"

"Get away from the door!" I screamed like Regan from *The Exorcist.*

"Okay, I'm sorry. Are you okay?"

toot *toot* *splatter* *ungodly noise*

"I'm fine, Rob—just leave the shoes there. I'll call you later, okay?"

"Okay, are you sure you're . . ."

"I'm fine! Get away from the door!"

This man! I love him, but take a freakin' hint.

Finally, I heard the front door shut and the Cobra engine zoom away. I thought that was the last I'd hear from him. I didn't think it was possible to ever hear from a man again if he had screamed that he could taste your fart after only knowing you for forty-eight hours.

But to my surprise, I did. A couple of days later, actually. Now we're married, and he's lying on the couch while I type this.

"It was your rack that saved you," he just lovingly reminded me.

Well, thank you, boobs. You saved us. You saved our destiny.

SEVEN

COUPLE'S MASSAGE

Valentine's Day was a lot more fun when I didn't share a bank account with my valentine. It's one of the few things I miss about dating. All those free drinks and meals! Receiving a huge bouquet of flowers without fearing I'd have to adjust the week's grocery budget to cover it! It was a wonderful chapter in my life.

Rob and I had only been dating a couple of months when he surprised me with a spa day and various little gifts. One gift was in a jewelry box. It was a thin little ring with a pink heart as the gem. It was thoughtful and sweet, but not my style—not even close. It was likely a Zales special but also looked like it could turn your finger green. This caused an awkward dance of pretending I adored it while never actually wearing it. After giving Rob a big hug and kiss, I slipped it on my finger. That afternoon was the last time the ring would see the light of day for at least a decade.

Every once in a while, Rob would ask, "Where's that ring I gave you for our first Valentine's Day?" and I'd run to my chest of drawers, dig around through various period panties and other miscellaneous items, and present the ring. Each time he'd follow up with, "How come you don't wear it?"

And each time I'd say, "Oh, a ring like this needs the right outfit."

That seemed to satisfy him, and back in the drawer it would go. Until years later on one fateful evening I got a little desperate.

I was lying in bed next to Lucy, humming and trying to soothe her to sleep.

"Mommy?" she said dreamily.

"Yes?"

"I can't wait to see what the tooth fairy gives me."

I froze. She'd lost her tooth earlier, and I'd forgotten.

She hadn't learned about the tooth fairy from me. I'm good with using our imaginations and enjoying delightful characters on holidays, but the tooth fairy has always struck me as high cost, low reward. On top of that, I found her hard to explain. Santa Claus was easy. The Easter bunny was weird, but Lucy was willing to look past it. The tooth fairy, however, held a fanciful story line I couldn't quite grasp. *She comes into my child's bedroom at night, steals her tooth for some reason, and replaces it with cash . . . why?* I have no idea where Lucy learned about T. fairy; all I know is that someone spilled the tea, and Lucy was looking to collect.

Earlier that day, she'd gotten right to business as soon as Rob yanked the tooth out of her mouth. He was still holding her tooth pinched between his fingers when she asked through her blood-soaked lips, "Does the tooth fairy come now?"

Rob and I stared at each other and blinked.

"Oh. Huh. Yes. The tooth fairy. Where'd you hear about the tooth fairy?" I asked. I'd hoped when it was my turn to have babies, the tooth fairy would've phased out.

"Dunno," she said with a shrug. "So what kinda surprise does she bring me?" Lucy watched while I put her tooth in a ziplock sandwich bag.

"She gives you a little bit of money, like a whole dollar!" I tried to hype it up since a dollar won't even get you a pack of Skittles these days.

"But what's money?"

"It's what grown-ups use to buy things."

"You don't use money. You use cards."

"Right, but those cards represent money." I was getting in the weeds and needed an exit. "Don't worry about all that. I'm sure she'll give you a little money you can save, and then we'll buy something next time we're at Target."

"But I don't want money. I want a unicorn ring!"

"What do you mean a unicorn ring?" My hand flipped to my hip. Lucy always does this. She gets weirdly specific at the worst times. "The tooth fairy only carries cash, baby. She doesn't take requests, okay? She's not like Santa. She gives you money. End of story."

I had to put the tooth fairy business on the back burner to make some phone calls. Worst-case scenario, I would just go to the ATM and withdraw cash after I put her to bed and then sneak into her room at some point.

The tasks I give myself for later in the day always feel like no big deal until it's actually time to do them. Then Later Anna curses Earlier Anna for giving her such a stupid, last-minute to-do list. Later Anna, however, always has the last laugh by refusing to do the things on the list. Or forgetting to do them. So it was no surprise I completely forgot about the tooth fairy nonsense until Lucy gently reminded me as she dozed off to sleep.

"I bet the tooth fairy will give me a unicorn ring," she said, reminding me of the ziplock bag under her pillow. To be honest, the ziplock bag kind of took the ambiance out of the whole thing. Like, it really needed to be in some envelope with a lovely little note that we would eventually keep in a precious scrapbook I updated monthly. But, sadly, I'm not that kind of mother, despite how often I try to force it. And besides—it was late, my bra was already off, and I still didn't know how I was going to get my hands on some cash.

I sped up my humming to get our nighttime ritual over and done with so I could figure out a plan. My mom hadn't been fully into the tooth fairy, but I do remember one time getting two whole dollars under my pillow. That was the '80s, though. I wondered if there had been tooth fairy inflation, and if so, how much? I kissed Lucy good night, then slipped out of her bed to google it. I found a large range of strong opinions, so I texted my friend who had older children. She responded:

I go to the bank and get Emma shiny $1 coins. I give her as many as her age, so for this last tooth she got 7 gold coins. She loved it.

I didn't even reply to that nonsense.

Was there something else I could give her? Did I have any cheap jewelry or cheap rings somewhere? My mind spun until *Aha! The heart ring!* Granted, it wasn't a unicorn ring, and it was definitely oversized, but it had a touch of whimsy, so I thought it might work. Besides, it was better than a ziplock bag of crusty pennies—one can hope.

After getting the ring from my drawer, I tiptoed back to Lucy's room, zipping with so much nervous energy I might as well have been sneaking past a sleepy security guard to rob a bank. I ever so slowly turned the door handle, flinching as it popped open much louder than necessary. I paused, with bated breath, before pushing the door open. It creaked as if I were opening a castle door to a witch's den. I winced and bit my lip as a sharp beam of light from the hallway cast directly onto her closed eyelids. Quickly, I scurried in, finally taking in tiny breaths so as not to pass out. She roused, just a little, but I was able to sneak the heart ring under her pillow without waking her.

I left her room, exhaling in relief, but wasn't in the clear. I might have been a little too fast and loose with Rob's sentimentality toward the ring, so I needed to conjure an explanation where I bore zero responsibility.

Rob was watching football in the living room, and I waltzed in with a nervous, faux pleasantness—as if I'd rear-ended his car and needed the right moment to come clean. "Well, I, um, solved the tooth fairy debacle," I said, sitting next to him. Then I pretended to flip through the *New Yorker*.

"Oh yeah? You find some cash somewhere?" he asked, changing the channel to another game.

"No, I, um, gave her one of my rings."

Rob had just been feigning interest to be polite, but now I had his full attention. "What ring?"

"Oh, um, you know. That ring with a heart on it. I've had it for years."

"The one I gave you when we were dating?" he asked, voice raised with a twinge of betrayal.

He left me no choice but to defend myself and make the whole thing his fault.

"Well, what was I supposed to do?" I said, tossing the *New Yorker* aside. "I spent my entire day stressed because I needed tooth fairy cash, and who wants to make a trip to the ATM? And then I gotta go break it for change? Who has time for this madness?" I was building momentum and leaned in. "And you're down here all relaxed, completely oblivious! Like, why is this all *my* responsibility? And now that I think about it, when's the last time you washed our bedding? I'm serious. When was the last time you stripped our bed and washed our sheets? I'll wait." I might have gone right off the rails with that one, but he'd gotten me all riled up, reminding me of the injustices I've endured in our marriage. "Besides," I went on, "it wasn't a diamond or anything. I figured it would be okay."

"But it wasn't cheap!"

I side-eyed him and pursed my lips.

"Well, it wasn't *that* cheap," he said with a sigh. "I guess it's fine. Think she'll lose it?" I was relieved when his temperature cooled. Still, I didn't have the heart to tell him that she would most definitely lose it. And of course, she did lose it, within two hours of waking. To this day, it's just gone, vanished. Probably hanging out with all our household's lost socks, Tupperware lids, ChapStick balms, and pens.

I'm not a very sentimental person, but I was a little sad when it disappeared. Lucy, who'd been thrilled to receive it, accepted its loss a little too easily in my opinion. It's not like I was going to wear it anytime soon, or ever at all, but I kind of liked having it in my drawer for safekeeping, protected by all those period panties, waiting for me to visit on a whim.

We had been so fresh and new in our relationship; it was obvious Rob was using our first Valentine's Day to go all in. We cuddled and shared classy chocolate-covered strawberries on a bench outside his apartment complex. The heart ring he had just given me was front and center on my finger as I made a move for the white chocolate strawberry. The ring kept catching my eye for all the wrong reasons, but it didn't dare spoil the fun. I felt so lovely and romantic and flushed with delight.

"We're going to be late for the massage appointment," he said, picking a chocolate shard off his shirt.

"What are you going to do while I get the massage?" I asked. "Wait in the lobby or something?"

"Oh, no," he said. "It's a couple's massage."

My entire body took a long pause. I viewed a couple's massage

89

as a thing you do at an all-inclusive Sandals resort on your honeymoon, and even then I'd rather not. I prefer to get my body worked in the presence of the person paid to do the rubbing, alone. It's an intimate experience. Any slight groans and gentle words expressed, like "Is that too hard?" and "Just a little," are between me and the highly trained professional.

We were just a handful of dates in and had only shared some smooches. Now we were going straight to the couple's massage? Weren't we skipping over a lot of things in between? Would soft flutes and wind chimes play on a stereo while we undressed in the same lavender-scented room? How would I feel as I listened to the guy I was dating getting his body rubbed down by a stranger? Was I expected to not laugh?

In each and every awkward situation in my life, I have always laughed. And once I start, I can't stop, making it even more awkward, sending me into a vicious laugh loop. In high school, sitting in math class, my friend was digging around in her bag for a pen and pulled out a tampon. No one saw it but me, and I braced while giggles rocked me like a hurricane. My teacher, Mr. Lemon, grew increasingly annoyed and threatened to send me to the dean's office. That scared me a little, but I was too far gone and eventually had to get up, grab my backpack, and take his pink slip.

"What'd you do?" the dean asked from behind his desk.

"I got the giggles," I said, sitting with my hands in my lap, my eyes puffy from tears of laughter. That sentence alone triggered them all over again. The dean had to sit and watch me as I laughed, silently yet uncontrollably, with my chin down at my neck, my hand waving him off. "I'm so sorry," I managed to get out, wiping my eyes. "So, so sorry."

And so it has always been.

I felt Rob might be setting us up for failure with this premature couple's massage, but what could I do about it? I suppose I could've declined, but that seemed a bit dramatic and probably a little hurtful since he seemed so sure and proud of himself. And besides, like sex and pizza, even a bad massage is good. I decided to remain positive and give it a go.

The building and decor looked very nice for a small-town spa. I expected it to be in some aging strip mall, but they had done their due diligence to create a peaceful, meditative, Buddha-like spa experience. The girl behind the counter was cheerful, her face round and red like a strawberry. She smiled sweetly, but her movements and tone were unnatural, as if it were her first day and she was trying incredibly hard to look like she knew what she was doing. Her face was freckled, and her bright-red hair was pulled into a tight ponytail. I zeroed in on how she appeared greased up and slippery. At first I thought she was sweaty, and she might have been, but it also appeared she'd gotten into the spa lotions and didn't know when to quit.

"Let me give you a tour," she said, slow and low, methodically like a robot. I had a sense she normally had a higher-pitched, bubbly voice but was forcing it down several octaves to match the tranquility of the wind chimes and waterfall sounds permeating the building. She waved her hand to the right, directing us down the hall. Her arm was stiff, and her fingers were pressed together like a Barbie hand. As we made our way down the hall, she took us to a room with a small waterfall in it. "This is our bamboo room," she said, so low and soft I had to duck my head down and squint real hard to catch what she was saying. "The entire room is made out of 100 percent sustainable, fair trade bamboo. No animals or humans were hurt in the harvesting of our bamboo in the bamboo room." I nodded and smiled. Rob looked annoyed.

She took us to see a mud bath area, a hot tub area, a facial area, and several other areas, until she eventually took us into our room, where two massage tables were near each other. "Please undress and get under the sheets. We will be in with you shortly," she said, arm jutted out and bent at the elbow as she exited the room. I made Rob turn around while I undressed. "If Strawberry Shortcake is one of the masseuses, you get her," I told him while racing to get my bra off so I could dive under the sheet as quickly as possible.

"Why? What's it matter?"

"What's it matter?" I said, my voice muffled through the face hole of my massage table. "She's awkward and unsure of herself. If a stranger is going to grease me up and rub me down, I want her confident and strong." Rob laughed to himself and got under the sheet. We gazed at each other for a little while.

"I hope you're having a good Valentine's Day," he said.

"I am." I smiled.

An older woman lightly knocked and came in. She looked confident and well seasoned, everything I could have hoped for. But she made her way over to Rob's table and put her hand on his back, quietly asking him questions out of my earshot. I was a little disappointed but held out hope I was going to get a confident and weathered masseuse of my own. Then Strawberry Shortcake walked in. She had changed out of her black T-shirt and yoga pants into black, Asian-style scrubs. She placed her hand near my nose and had me smell various essential oils to pick out my favorite. They all smelled good, so having to choose just one stressed me out. I landed on eucalyptus just to get it over with. She turned to get the supplies arranged, bumping her hip into my shoulder. "Ope," she said with a giggle.

Ugh. Why me? My dissatisfaction wasn't personal—I'm just incredibly picky about who will be rubbing their hands all over my naked body, occasionally grazing my butt crack. But I didn't want to nitpick on superficial things, like that bamboo spiel or the stiff arms, the unnaturally low tone or the way she was over-greased. A massage is a massage, after all.

But is it really?

This wouldn't be the last time Rob booked me a disappointing massage. Several years later, he'd surprise me by booking one after I had a stressful week. "Your original appointment was with some Mark guy, but I had it changed to a woman."

"Really?" I said, surprised at his insecurity. "That's not like you to be jealous. They're all professionals." Of course, so was Strawberry, but she didn't count.

"I don't want no dude rubbing my babe down," he said matter-of-factly. And that was the end of that.

I arrived at the salon a little early and took a seat, flipping through an old *People* magazine. A man emerged from the back and immediately caught my attention. He looked like David Beckham—the kind of hot that gets you so flustered that you start stuttering and dropping things and pitting out your shirt. The girls behind the counter immediately changed their demeanor when he walked in, giggling and posing and not totally sure what to do with their hands. The name tag on his shirt read "Mark."

Probably for the best. I sighed, mindlessly flipping through pages. *I'm married, after all.*

As I was called back, I remained open-minded and hopeful as to who Mark's replacement would be. I undressed and got under the sheet. Soon after, an older woman came in. She didn't put on any airs by using a soft, gentle tone. She spoke loudly and was direct. Almost inappropriately so. "You Anna?" she asked, coming around the side of my table.

"Yes?"

"I'm Sheila. Nice to meet ya." Her nose sounded stuffed, like she had a cold, and she was aggressively working around a throat lozenge in her mouth. All the open-mouth breathing, smacking, and lozenge-to-teeth clacking had me feeling defeated before the massage even began. She placed a jar near my nose so I could choose which essential oils I wanted to use, but I couldn't smell anything over the overwhelming scent of Bengay wafting from her hands. I was so disappointed I just said, "Whatever. The first one's fine," and lay limp and sorry for myself. I could have had Mark! And here I was with a poor elderly woman with a cold, who undoubtedly had very sore, arthritic hands lathered in Bengay because of, I'm sure, a grueling massage schedule. I came for stress relief, not to participate in elder abuse!

To Sheila's credit, she gave me a nice, firm, and relaxing massage. But as I walked through the small lobby to leave, I met eyes with Mark, who was at the counter, greeting his next appointment. He nodded and gave me a smile, and I gave him one in return. Sure, my massage with Bengay Sheila was pretty good, but I couldn't help but wonder what might have been.

And this, for the most part, is how things eventually played out with Strawberry Shortcake. The massage felt nice, and she even surprised me with a few satisfying rubs. But if it's not one thing, it's another. My relaxation was rudely interrupted by a low moan. Like someone was hurt, but hurt so good. Listen, I barely enjoy massages as it is. It's not because they don't feel good—they always feel good. It's mostly because I'm so busy anticipating the ending that I'm barely able to enjoy the massage while it's happening. So while I was grieving the end of my massage less than halfway through, I had to also endure the sound of Rob moaning while getting massaged. Who does that with another person in the room? And worse, it kept happening, while his masseuse continued to encourage him through it. I guess he had a knot or something, but how is that my problem? *Why are we in the same room, Rob?!*

I tried to reel it in and focus. "Feel the massage. Focus on the massage," I chanted to myself. But it was too late. As Rob let out yet another self-indulgent moan, and as his older masseuse gently guided him through what sounded like both physical and emotional pain, the giggles began to emerge from the depths of my soul. I took deep breaths, trying everything I could to stop them from rising. But it was no use; it never is. My whole body began to shake as I used all my strength to fight back the quake of laughter.

"Are you okay?" Strawberry asked, concerned.

"I'm sorry," I muttered into the face hole.

"What's that?" she asked.

I started to shake thunderously, waving her off, trying everything I could to stop the inevitable.

"I'm sorry," I strained to say, as my body convulsed on the table. "It's him, the moaning." I waved her off, trying to catch precious breaths, but to the layman's eye, I appeared to be seizing. Growing more concerned, she put her head near mine.

"I'm sorry, hun. What are you saying?"

"I'm fine, I'm just laughing. It's the giggles. I'm sorry. It's not you. I'm so sorry."

Strawberry went back to working my upper thigh meat, I assume not knowing what else to do. Mercifully, my giggles eventually rolled to a stop, just as it was time to roll onto my back.

"Okay, go ahead and roll over. I'll hold the sheet for you," Strawberry said. I slowly rolled over and we unfortunately made eye contact. She giggled in response, the same giggle a teddy bear would let out if you squeezed its paw, and it disturbed me greatly.

Strawberry moved toward my head and started working my neck. She found a kink and gave it some pressure. "Is that too hard?" she asked in her low, pretend masseuse voice.

"Just a little," I said back. She eased up slightly. I glanced at Rob, who was completely blissed out, unaware I was even in the room. I didn't know for sure, but I had a hunch I would know that man for the rest of my life.

"I like your ring," Strawberry said gently. I was of half a mind to slip it off my hand and give it to her, but I wouldn't dare. Rob had given it to me, and that alone gave me a warm feeling—the peaceful kind of warmth when joy is brewing. The fact I wouldn't be caught dead wearing it again was irrelevant.

My mind wandered as Strawberry pressed onto my greased-up body. Rob moaned again under the firm hands of an older woman. Then, out of nowhere, the giggles came back round the bend.

I braced, but it was far too late. There was no use stopping the inevitable.

WHOLE FOODS
LINDA

I had asked the butcher for a pound and a half of stew meat when she caught my eye. She was with her teenage daughter, standing by the pasture-raised hot dogs. She tried to be discreet with her tears, but it was too late—at least for her daughter, who just stood there, eyes darting around looking desperately for an exit. Her mom was talking to Linda, sniffling and smiling and nodding her head, while Linda cupped the woman's hand with her own. Linda's hands were speckled in age spots and bumpy with veins, but love flowed through her fingertips.

Linda was tiny. She couldn't have been more than five feet tall and a hundred pounds. She made you want to take her into your arms, delicately, like an injured little bird.

She had cancer, although she never provided specifics on if she was going through treatment or slowly dying, and it never seemed polite to ask. Colorful scarves adorned her head, underneath a large sunbonnet. It wasn't until much later that I discovered Linda didn't actually know the crying woman. She had just bumped into her, near the pasture-raised hot dogs, and said the words she felt compelled to say. Whatever she said, it brought the woman to tears, the same way your lip trembles when someone gently, lovingly, speaks to your pain so you don't have to.

Linda would walk around Whole Foods every Saturday morning around ten o'clock, pushing an empty cart. Once in a while there would be a cantaloupe rolling about. One time, a large rump roast. I remember that only because I hoped it meant she had an appetite.

My mom and I would meet at Whole Foods every Saturday to grocery shop together and make an experience out of it. I mean, if this is something you have to do each week, why not enjoy it? Sometimes we'd get a bottle of wine and a cheese plate, but those were usually the shopping trips where all I'd come home with was a take-and-bake pizza and a ten-dollar tube of all-natural toothpaste.

On this day, we were sitting at a high top, drinking coffee and flipping through a *Cook's Illustrated* together, when Linda strolled past, pushing her empty cart. I recognized her as the little old lady who had held the crying woman's hand by the pasture-raised hot dogs, but didn't think much of it. "Hold on, honey. I want to introduce you to someone," my mom said, hopping off her chair.

I sighed and put the magazine down. I was having a bad day. I had hired someone to help me grow my website, and we hadn't made it six months before I had to cut her loose. Lies were being spread, impacting my personal and professional relationships, and I was enraged in the most sorrowful way. But I tried as best I could to stuff it all down, and now I was at Whole Foods, sipping my coffee and pretending to look at a *Cook's Illustrated.*

"Linda, this is my daughter Anna," my mom said, gently guiding her by the elbow toward the table.

"Hello," I said with a half smile.

"Anna's a little blue today," Mom went on. "She had to make a hard decision, and we've been working through it."

"Oh, hun, don't even worry about it," Linda said, flipping her hand at me. "You're better off without her. That girl had emotional problems."

My eyes flashed wide. "Wait. Did you tell? How did . . . did . . ."

"So what do you do, sweetheart?" She took my hand and held it between her soft, fragile ones.

"I'm a humor writer, and I run a funny website for women," I said. The answer was simple enough, but my voice cracked. I felt like she knew things about me, could really see me, and everything would be just fine.

"Oh? And what's your website called? I'll look it up when I get home! My son gave me one of those iPads. I'm pretty good at it!"

When Jen recommended I call my funny new website for women "HaHas for HooHas," I went with it because we couldn't think of anything funnier, and I never anticipated all the times I'd have to awkwardly share it with elderly people.

"Well, the name is kind of crude." I laughed nervously.

"Try me."

"HaHas for . . . HooHas?"

Linda laughed, and it was genuine too. I'm always relieved when I don't have to explain the joke because it never goes well. *HooHas is basically a slang term for vaginas, so it's "HaHas for HooHas" like "Funny for Vaginas," or women, actually. It's like, "Laughs for Women" or whatever. Ahem. So, what do you do?*

"I want you to come to my Bible study on Wednesday nights and read us your stories. Some of these women really need to lighten up," Linda said, waving her hand.

I would have loved to, but my latest essay was called "Big Boob Problems," which went into great detail about how I fear emergencies, not because I fear for my life but because of the repetitive hard boob claps that are sure to follow suit as I flee a burning building. So even though I had no doubt some of those ladies needed to lighten up, I hoped maybe we could just play it by ear.

She turned her attention to my mom, and as they chatted, Linda said, "Christine, I see some African ancestors and a Jewish mantle above you. Do you know your ancestry?"

My mom is 100 percent Sicilian. We long assumed we had African ancestors in our lineage, but we also suspected we had Jewish lineage too. This was getting weird. I felt all fuzzy, like something supernatural was happening, and I didn't know how to stand or where to put my hands.

After a few more pleasantries, she hugged us both as if we were two rare, precious jewels and pushed her empty cart away to find someone else to speak lovingly to until they burst into tears.

"What was that about?" I asked my mom, hoisting my butt back on the high chair. "Did you talk to her about my business?"

"No! Of course not. It's a gift," Mom said. "She has an intuition. Isn't she wonderful?"

I didn't think that kind of thing was real-life. As a Christian woman, I knew there were many spiritual gifts—and some were a little intense, like talking in tongues. But this was next-level.

Linda wasn't psychic. If she were to explain her gift, she'd simply say, "God gives me insights on his children, so I try to make myself available for him to love them as often as I can." Or, more specifically, at Whole Foods around ten o'clock in the morning.

Obviously, this gift gave Linda quite the reputation. In fact, if you told someone who knew Linda that you ran into her, they'd get all worked up and make it about them. "*Linda*, Linda? What did she say? I need a good word! Did she give you a good word about me?"

And then you'd have to say, "Oh gosh, no. I'm sorry—you never came up. I really tried to keep the conversation on me the entire time." Then they'd be all disappointed and wouldn't care to listen to what else you had to say.

In fact, Linda became so in demand that she refused to give out her phone number. I know because I tried to get it. "Oh, honey," she said, patting my hand. "If I gave my number to people, it'd ring off the hook." She wasn't there to make needy friends.

She had a job to do, and she was willing to show up at Whole Foods at ten o'clock every Saturday morning to do it. Beyond that, we were on our own. She had cancer, for heaven's sake!

When I got home, I threw my groceries on the kitchen island and told Rob all about Linda. "She encouraged me specifically about my business partnership ending, even though I never said a word about it!" I was shouting at this point, and he was watching a college basketball game, feigning interest but mostly turning up the volume secretly. I started to get all sorts of ideas, like maybe I could casually bump into her with Rob and she could give *him* a good word. If anyone needed a good word, it was Rob.

At the time, he was about to graduate from nursing school and had just realized he would rather die than be a nurse. I wouldn't say it was an unhappy time in our marriage, but he was low-key unhappy most of the time. He felt like he had racked up school loans for a career he never really wanted, and he had an underlying despair about him I hoped Linda could shake loose.

The following Saturday, I talked Rob into coming with me to the grocery store. Mom couldn't make it, so we sat together at our own high top. I had an iced coffee, Rob had a latte, and I could tell he was wondering how he got talked into this crap on his one day off.

"Come on, Linda," I whispered, scanning the crowds. "Don't let me down now!"

Finally, a cluster of shoppers departed, revealing Linda's tiny frame standing by her empty cart while she chatted with a family.

"There she is!" I grabbed Rob's arm.

"There who is?"

"Linda!"

"Who's Linda?"

"*Linda*, Linda—the one who's prophetic or whatever. Come on. Let me introduce her to you and see if we can get you a good word!" I jumped off my chair and made my way toward her, trying to act casual as if this were such a delightfully unexpected surprise. As I approached, she looked at me kindly.

"Oh, hi, Linda," I said as if we were long-lost friends. "So good to—"

"Well now, here's the young woman who's going to be on TV," she said, with her arms open for a hug.

"Wait, what?"

"Hi, I'm Rob," Rob said, jutting out his hand.

"Not now, Rob. I'm talking to Linda," I said as I moved into her arms. "I'm sorry, what did you say about me being on TV?"

"Well, hello! You must be Anna's husband?" She pulled away and reached her hand out to Rob.

I slapped Rob's hand down. "Excuse me, sorry, what did you say about me?"

"Yes, I am," Rob said with a smile. He went in for a hug (little presumptuous, in my opinion), then hovered, like a bellboy waiting for a tip.

"Oh, how nice," Linda said. "So good to meet you. So good to see you both. The rib eye is on sale!" Then she turned her attention back to the family.

Rob and I just stood there, grinning like idiots. Eventually, the awkwardness crowded us out, and we walked away.

"That's it?" Rob said.

"She's not the Long Island Medium, Rob. Stop trying to make it about you." I was chewing the edge of my thumbnail with an elevated heart rate. "Did you hear her say I was going to be on TV? What do you think she meant by that?" But Rob had stopped caring and made his way to the pizza bar.

For days I couldn't get her TV comment out of my mind. For the next few weeks I'd let my mind drift to what kind of TV show I was destined to be on. Perhaps my own Food Network show? I could hold my own in the kitchen, but I was no Anne Burrell. Still, if Ree Drummond could get her own show, why couldn't I? Maybe I'd be the new host of *Diners, Drive-Ins and Dives*—because, and I think we can all agree, America has had quite enough of Guy Fieri.

As the days went on, daily life demanded I obsess a bit less about my future in TV. Of course, that's right when the call came. I wrote a column for the *Omaha World-Herald*, and my editor asked me to join her on a local morning show spot. It was some biweekly thing she did as a parenting segment. She hated doing it and hoped to pawn it off on me. I agreed because I had nothing better to do, but I wasn't excited or anything. As far as I knew, the only people who watched the show were local nursing home residents, people awaiting surgery in hospitals, and my Aunt Mimi. I started to fry some eggs, when the realization gripped me. *Oh no. What if this is the TV appearance Linda was talking about?*

Surely when Linda had called me "the young woman who's going to be on TV" she hadn't meant "the young woman who will make a one-minute appearance on a local morning show no one watches—except for Aunt Mimi," right?

Right, Linda?

I called my mom for reassurance. "Anna, Linda isn't some oracle," she said. "She has an intuition that she uses to bless people. Let's not pervert her inten—" I hung up. I didn't need that kind of negativity in my life. The only way to get clarity was to get to the source: Linda.

But Linda stopped showing up. Every Saturday Mom and I went to Whole Foods for our regular shopping trip, and each time she wasn't there. I would scoff at the price of organic Honeycrisp apples, then look around, hoping Linda would emerge with her empty cart. I wanted her to hold my hand. To see me. And tell me I was going to be the wildly famous regular on a new national TV show. If not Food Network, perhaps NBC? I wasn't picky. But mostly, I just wanted to be seen by Linda's loving, knowing gaze. On a top-rated TV show.

After a few months went by, Mom and I started to fear the worst. Had her health gotten worse? Could she have died? It was awful not knowing. I didn't know her well at all, but she felt familial to me, as if I had always known her. Maybe she was a glimpse of heaven you can't articulate—you simply know it when you see it. I had just begun to accept I wouldn't see her again when I looked up from my grocery list and there she was. Pushing her empty cart, loving on people. "Mom!" I shouted across the olive bar. "It's Linda! She's not dead!" Mom dropped the Irish soda bread she was eyeing and came running.

She greeted us with warmth and kindness. Linda admitted to having some health problems but now felt very good. We exchanged our pleasantries and tight hugs. There was no good word that day, but as it turned out, I didn't need one. I just enjoyed being in her presence, without expectation. It's quite a gift when you can take someone wrapped up in their feels—all their doom and gloom—and, with just a few words, make them realize it's not that serious. That, although it may not feel like it now, life's so much better this way. Without even trying, she gave me peace and confidence that all will be, and must be, well.

I never saw Linda again.

To be honest, I don't actually know if she's dead or just goes to Whole Foods on Tuesdays now. So, if you're still alive and happen to read this, Linda—sorry for the mix-up. But in my defense, you never let me have your phone number.

NINE

FRANCES WITH THE GOOD SALINE

How do I describe it? I guess it looked like a vintage TV that had just been turned off. The screen went black, but there was a white dot in the center that remained there a few moments. That's the first thing I remember. Then the dot grew, like I was looking through a cardboard toilet paper tube.

I could see my finger—I was pointing. And I could see the faces of two women come into the circle of my vision. I was talking, loudly. *What am I saying, and why am I saying it with so much enthusiasm?* I wondered.

"I like you!" I shouted, before pivoting my finger at the next poor nurse, "I like *you*! And I *really* like YOU!" The last declaration seemed to shake loose my consciousness and bring it back into semialignment with my cognitive awareness.

"Was I talking out loud?" I quickly asked no one in particular.

"Yep," one of them replied, with a slight twinge of annoyance in her voice. None of the nurses were particularly nice. They seemed busy and put out, as if they all had endured the longest day and in the final fifteen minutes of their shift I had gone and crapped my pants.

The toilet paper tube had fully widened, and I was aware but just couldn't shut up. Aides were now bringing another man into the room, and I started piecing fragments together. I was recovering from surgery and was coming down from what appeared to be the best high of my life. I was now in a post-op room with a few other recovering patients.

"Okay, Bob," one of the aides said, "you're all set. A nurse will come check on you in a minute."

"Hey, Bob!" I shouted, completely against my own will. "Bob!"

A weak, shaky voice spoke. "Is someone saying my name?"

"Bob! Over here!"

"It's another patient in the room," the aide assured Bob, his tone also nonplussed.

"Bob, Bob!" I saw my leg kick up into my view as if it were some prop thrust onstage. I was surprised to see I was wearing bright-orange compression socks and ecstatic to see Bob wearing the same. "Nice socks," I told him, pursing my lips, wiggling my foot, and rapidly raising my eyebrows.

"What'd she say?" frail little Bob muttered.

"She said 'nice socks.' Just ignore her," the aide said, fussing around Bob's bed. I mean, I get it. I'm a little annoying, but they were all just being rude.

Rob, once also a nurse, assures me everyone's put-off vibes aren't personal. They aren't grumpy; they're just no-nonsense because PACU nurses spend their entire days dealing with people temporarily out of their minds. After this surgery experience, I shared some of it on my Facebook page. I apparently have a robust following of nurses, and all of them tried to help soothe my fears.

> **AMBER:** Oh, that's nothing. I had a woman come out of surgery and cup the doctor's jewels.
>
> **KRISTEN:** You're fine. At least you weren't honking their boobs like most people do.
>
> **TARA:** People say the filthiest things coming out of surgery, it's hilarious! Men, women, young and old. It's just part of the job.

At first I felt relief that crazy behavior was common. But this realization led to more terrifying questions: (1) Why is everyone so horny coming out of surgery? And (2) what was I doing during the parts I can't remember? *Please, Lord, tell me I wasn't honking boobs and wieners!*

Since Bob was no fun, I tried settling down into my bed, but a burn was growing in my lower abdomen and started ruining my buzz. Another nurse made her way into my view. She was talking to me about buttons I could press and blah blah blah. I wasn't listening. "What's your pain level now, from one to ten?" she asked, pointing at a chart that had a series of round smiley faces ranging from delighted to actively being dismembered.

"Twelve," I said in full confidence. "The pain is bad. Really, really bad."

"Okay, so, ten is 'my arm has just been cut off,'" the nurse began (again with the tone!), "so with that in mind, where we at now?"

"Oh. A three?"

The nurse left, I assume to log in pain meds appropriate for a level three, and it all started coming back to me, like waking up with a hangover and getting snapshots of the night before. *Snap!* Trying to kiss the guy in a tank top with hairy shoulders. *Snap!* Peeing in the front yard. *Snap!* Crying uncontrollably in the back of an Uber because your Taco Bell order is missing the Doritos Locos. (In your defense, the Doritos Locos were the only reason you picked Taco Bell in the first place.)

I had been at the hospital all morning. When I first arrived, I was put into a room that was small but decorated like a hotel room. My mom sat at my side. Rob was at work, at the VA, and had begged to be with me. But he was out of sick days, and we were broke. He didn't care about the incoming reduced paycheck, but I did. I assured him I'd be fine, and I was. I was with my mom and felt good about it. Years later he'd admit that it was traumatic for him to be at work that day, away from me. I should have encouraged him to come, but honestly, I just wanted to get it done and over with. I was exhausted picking up my broken pieces, keeping them huddled close enough together that I was still some semblance of myself. I didn't have enough hands for his too.

A lovely older woman came in and introduced herself as Frances. She was cheerful and calm, prepping me for surgery.

I loved saying her name and tried fitting it in wherever I could. "Hey, Frances, you a fan of *The Pioneer Woman*, Frances?" I asked, motioning toward the TV.

"Oh, I don't know," she said, making her way around the bed. "I like her show, but sometimes she's too cute for her own good. Have you read her blog recipes? Who's got time to scroll through a photo series of browning ground beef?" Frances put an IV port into my hand and connected it to a bag hanging from the IV pole. I immediately succumbed to a whoosh of warmth and felt myself slowly melting into the bed.

"Woah, Frances. I feel it already," I purred. "What's the street name for this?"

"Oh, hun, that's just saline solution."

Frances left Mom and me to ourselves as we continued to wait. I was in good spirits, but I was hammering my mom over the head with nonstop one-liners. She was having the time of her life, don't get me wrong, but relentless jokes aren't typically a sign I'm in a great mood; it means I'm nervous.

The anesthesiologist came in next. He was tall with a thick accent I didn't recognize. He was also freaky handsome—like a model in an ad you'd see ten stories tall in Times Square. He introduced himself as Dr. Tom. Like Frances's, his tone was gentle, cheerful, and calm—and I started to wonder if they're trained that way since most of us are sad and scared.

Legally, he had to go over the procedure and worst possible outcomes. He flipped through paperwork I would have to sign and assured me of how safe the anesthesia was and that he would be there the entire time should anything out of the ordinary happen.

"You may have stroke. But no, no, no, no. You young. You healthy." He turned the page. "You may have heart attack. Nonsense. You young. Your heart strong. Very, very rare. Heart attack? No way, no, no, no, no, no."

As he made his way through the legal talking points, I sank deep into the mattress with dread. I sensed the initial stages of the giggles arriving, approaching fast. The lighthearted, encouraging way he listed all the gruesome ways I might die, mixed in with that good saline just hittin' different, led me near the cliff's edge. Having my mom there amplified my deep desire to just laugh, uncontrollably, forever. But it would be weird and disrespectful, and the poor doctor just wanted to get through this very important nonsense and move on with his life. I bit my lower lip, then drew deep, long breaths, attempting a meditative state.

"You may stop breathing, but it's okay! I right there. I take care of you and make sure nothing bad happen," he said, flipping to the last page. "Any questions?"

I managed to squeak out the words, "Nope, that about covers it," as I signed away rights for my heart to stop beating without threat of litigation. He shut the door behind him, and I launched into a full stand-up routine.

"You can't sleep? Don't worry, I rock you like baby. You die? I pump your heart with my two soft hands." Mom's laugh stopped making sound, her eyeliner streaking down her cheeks. Just then, my doctor performing the procedure, Dr. Collins, came in. "Wow, we're having some fun in here, aren't we? What's so funny?"

"Oh, I'm just making my mom laugh."

"She was imitating Dr. Tom," my mom said, taking big swipes underneath her eyes to wipe away mascara-covered tears. I shot Mom with "that's supposed to be between us" eyes.

"Oh yeah? That had to be good. Let me hear it," Dr. Collins said.

See, here's the thing. Dr. Tom was wonderful. He was gentle, soothing, and used light humor to help me during an extremely difficult time. If you were in the room from start to finish, you'd know I was simply poking fun at poor Dr. Tom being forced to go over all the gruesome ways I might die with his delightful reassurances that all was well, his lovely accent tying it all together with a bow. But to outsiders, there was a high probability I'd sound disrespectful at best and a tad prejudiced at worst. Mostly because I'm really bad at accents. It doesn't matter if it's English, Australian, French, Nigerian, or Southern, I eventually go Asian. It's not intentional; I simply lack talent, but who would ever believe me? Even my husband struggles. Lost in a wicked binge of *The Crown*, I was relaying a scene of Queen Elizabeth to him after he'd just gotten back from the bathroom. "Why do you sound like Jackie Chan?" he asked, trying to not be troubled. I wish I could tell you, friends. I wish I could tell you.

"Oh no, I can't. It was silly," I said, praying Dr. Collins would just drop it already.

"Oh, come on," she playfully pushed. Just then a couple aides came in to start pushing my bed out into surgery. "Yeah, just grab the ends there," she directed. "You feeling okay, Anna? Feeling ready?" she asked, rubbing my foot gently.

Relieved to move on, I smiled. "Yes, I'm ready. I know it will go just fine."

"All right, let's go then," she said, before redirecting to my mom. "They'll call you in when she's all done, Mom. You can go back to the waiting area." Then turning back to me she said, "But seriously, let me hear your Dr. Tom impression." Oh, this woman! I love her, but let it go!

You can only resist retelling a story so many times before resisting becomes more painful than just giving the people what they want. "Well, um, okay," I cleared my throat. "You heart stop? No! You healthy! You young! I make it beat again with my own two hands. You stop breathing? I right there; I fill your lungs with fresh breeze of flapping angel's wings." Everyone laughed, including the aides, which surprised me because the angel wings bit was a little clumsy.

"That's good!" Dr. Collins said. "He has a great sense of humor; he'd love that." I took a deep breath. As they pushed me down the hall, I gazed at the white hospital ceiling tiles, some with brown stains from what must have been a leaky roof. Bright fluorescent lights went past, on rhythm. No more noise, no more performing, no more Frances with the good saline. I could feel it now. I was scared. The aides wheeled me into the surgical room and brought me to a stop. People fiddled all around me; tubes were injected into my IV port. "Dr. Tom!" Dr. Collins said gleefully. "Anna has a great impression of you!"

Oh no. Oh no, no, no. no, no.

"Oh yeah?" he said. "Let's hear it!"

"Oh, um, no, it's silly. Please."

"Oh, come on, I want to hear the impression," he said, so handsome, so trusting.

"Okay, um . . . Your heart stop? I pump it back to life! You have stroke? . . ." And then, just like that, someone turned off the TV.

If I could leave you with one solid piece of advice, it's this: don't fall in love with your doctor. The feeling's not mutual. This is easier said than done. If every time we meet we're either talking about my vagina or looking inside my vagina, intimacy is taking place. Sure, I may just be your ten o'clock cervix check, but to me it's something more. You're my trusted medical professional. You know me, sort of. I know you, not really at all. But we're bonding, and we're friends, right?

It had been a few weeks since I had the D&C, the medical procedure that removed the remnants of my ectopic pregnancy. And I'd spent those few weeks terrified I had either offended or sexually harassed Dr. Tom while rousing from anesthesia. That was my third miscarriage in a row. I was getting weighed in at a follow-up appointment when I heard Dr. Collins's nurse practitioner, Wendy, with another patient. In the beginning of each pregnancy, I would rotate between seeing Dr. Collins and Wendy and came to adore them both. I loved Dr. Collins because she hadn't a speck of arrogance, pretentiousness, or that attitude some doctors have where they treat you like an idiot if you question their authority. She was compassionate, steady, and didn't sweat the small stuff. Best of all, she was hopeful. She would often come into the exam room wearing scrubs, with a messy ponytail, approachable and patient as I sifted through printed-out mommy blogs about the deadliness of epidurals so we could discuss the merit of that argument at length.

Wendy, on the other hand, was sassy. Cutting, with a great sense of humor. She, too, was compassionate, but a bit more no-nonsense. Wendy wore knee-high boots and smelled good. But most importantly, she laughed at my jokes. I saw her more often in the initial stages of the pregnancies I would eventually miscarry, and we had been through a lot together. Naturally I assumed we were close. That's when I heard her having a conversation in another room that sounded happy, friendly.

Perhaps a little *too friendly.*

In fact, I'd say she treated her patient exactly like she treated me. And then she laughed. Hard. As I was getting my blood pressure checked, I asked the nurse, "Oh, is Wendy with a friend or sister or something?"

"What? Um, no—that's another patient," the nurse said, counting beats.

"Oh," I said coldly.

"Hmm. Your blood pressure is a little high. Let's try it again," she said, peeling off the Velcro.

I thought Wendy and I had something special. I thought I made her laugh and we just, you know, connected. I waited in the exam room for Wendy to come in and wasn't feeling so jovial. Why give her a laugh when they're clearly a dime a dozen? I tried to give her the vibe things weren't cool between us, but she didn't even notice. It hadn't really occurred to me until that moment—she was seeing other patients.

I would become pregnant a year later with my fourth pregnancy. Experiencing multiple miscarriages over the course of four years was like watching water swish back and forth in a tube. On one end, I recognized that I was experiencing a very unfortunate but common process in creating other humans. And then, *swoosh*—despair. The fourth pregnancy, however, showed some promise. I had made it past week eight, a milestone I had never reached before. But one morning, I woke up with a ferocious migraine. Each of my miscarriages had started with one, and a few days later, after the headache had gone, so had my baby. Feeling the migraine grow in intensity coincided with the terror of yet another loss, but it all somehow intertwined with a familiar sense of redundancy and boredom. I had been here before. I was scared. I was exhausted. What else was new?

My pregnancy migraines felt like my eyes were going to burst out of my head and splatter on the walls. This one was especially bad, and I found myself in a vicious cycle of vomiting every fifteen minutes. Wendy wanted me to come in immediately and met me in a darkened exam room thirty minutes later, as I held my heavy, thumping head in my hands.

"Oh, I love this," she said, smiling. I lifted my head slowly and peeked at her through one cracked eye.

"Huh?"

"This means we have all sorts of hormones revving up, just what we need for this pregnancy."

"No," I said, dropping my head back into my hands. "Migraines are always the beginning of a miscarriage. I'm losing the baby." I started to cry, but it hurt so bad I just whimpered instead.

"Why don't we go take a look and see for ourselves. What do you say?"

I slowly followed her into a room with an ultrasound machine. You could tell she hadn't run one in a while and started poking at it. Eventually it behaved in a recognizable way, and after gooping up my belly, she moved the wand around. I saw her immediately. My precious little Lucy, with a big, rounded head, a protruding torso like a sea horse, and the skinniest twiggy little legs, pumping furiously like she was fleeing the cops on paddleboat.

"Well now, that doesn't look like a miscarriage to me," Wendy said gently.

I laughed my way into sobs and put my hands to my bulging, throbbing eyes so they wouldn't pop out. I had suffered and grieved, and now there she was, growing just as she was supposed to. And better still, showing promise that she wouldn't inherit my corn-dog legs. I got off the exam table, and Wendy hugged me.

As I was about to leave, I turned to speak. "Can I get your phone number?" I nearly asked, but I thought better of it. It's unwise to fall too in love with your doctor. It's for the best, I suppose. I had other loves in my life, and the circumference was growing. Rob and I held hands back to the car. I closed my thumping eyes as we drove back home and dreamed of those twiggy, busy little legs. I'd been drifting in and out of sleep when Rob nudged my arm. "Hey," he said softly, "I got you a little something." He handed me a cold chocolate milkshake.

"Whoa, Frances," I purred. "This is *good*. What's the street name for this?"

"It's called a Frosty. From Wendy's," Rob said. "And don't call me Frances."

I lay my head back and looked out the window, seeing all the same houses, gas stations, and street signs, as well as the same offensive pile of dog poop on the sidewalk I'd noticed on our drive in. But I had the sensation that I had never been here before. Like life had been renewed. Or I was new. Brighter maybe? Who can say? Maybe it was just that zingy feeling you get when you realize that from that moment on, things will never be the same.

TEN

STEVE BUSCEMI EYES

I asked my husband to help remove the pillow from my right side. Confused, he informed me there was no pillow. The gigantic, fluffy white thing I was referring to was actually my exposed right thigh.

Oh God, no. No, no, no, no, no. I was immediately struck with terror and disbelief. I had just binged on a *My 600-lb Life* marathon, and several parallels were emerging. There I was, bed-ridden, barking out orders at my husband. This pregnancy had turned me into a woman I no longer recognized. While it's true I've never been enthusiastic about my thighs, especially when catching my reflection in department store mirrors, at least I'd been mobile without assistance and hadn't needed my husband to wash my hidden crevices with a warm cloth. I wanted to enjoy this day of my delivery, but it was impossible now. *Look at my thighs!*

Feeling fat has ruined special occasions for women since the beginning of time. From fancy soirees thrown by Marie Antoinette to weddings, countless nights out, and Weight Watchers weigh-ins. After covering my exposed thigh with a stiff hospital blanket, my mind started to wander to other things, like this one time when my gay friend Erick and I were getting dressed in our hotel room and he talked me into a maxi dress with a loud yellow floral print. I had reservations, but he was so enthusiastic that I got wrapped up in all the hype. The high carried me all the way to the lobby of the Mirage, where I caught my reflection on its shiny walls. I immediately recognized my *nonna* from the old country, wearing her house muumuu and bright-red lipstick. I won't say feeling fat ruined Vegas for me, but it did steal my good humor. Now it was coming for my birth experience.

I wanted to be a real feminist about the whole thing. I knew in my heart how terrible it was to worry about how fat I looked when I was about to birth a baby, but I just couldn't get over it. I was in shock over what the pregnancy hormones and all that extra queso had done to me over the previous nine months. My entire being wanted to focus on the occasion and not my gigantic watermelon boobs rolling all around my belly. Wasn't the baby coming out the other end? Give me my integrity; hand me my bra!

Of course, it didn't help that the epidural was put on a little thick, and I couldn't move from the chest down. This must've triggered the cascade of self-loathing. I kept telling the nurse, "Listen, I know I'm new here, but surely I shouldn't feel like a quadriplegic, right?" I was just splatted out on display like one of those polar bears at the zoo who look like they know there's more to life than this crap, watching HGTV's *Rehab Addict* while people cycled in and out, looking at screens, pressing buttons, and, I can only assume, side-eyeing my thighs.

"Better too much than too little," the nurse said, handing me another Italian ice.

At one point she tried to get me to roll over onto my side so she could put an exercise ball between my knees and get a little momentum going. She was an older, tiny woman, and her struggle was sad to watch. Like someone unable to pull up her friend dangling off a cliff. I could tell she was defeated and running out of options. Just then Rob came back from a cafeteria run and was invited to help. Even my own six-foot-three husband struggled way too much for my liking. No woman wants a man to handle her and start sweating from the brow. To make matters worse, he began chastising me for not helping him. "Use your arms and pull, Anna!"

"I am using my arms!" I bellowed. *Who the hell put this idiot in charge? Get me a professional!*

This was not the beautiful birth experience I had imagined.

Once I was finally on my side, I slipped into a minidepression about the whole thing. Rob asked if I wanted him to move the bed around so I could at least see how the episode of *Rehab Addict* ended, but I was in no mood. Plus, you can only watch a woman decorate a powder room in black and white tile so many times. "Don't bother," I told him and stared out the window to a view of a parking garage.

I wondered if my worst fears about epidurals had come true. I had done my research, which mostly involved weird forums where commenters with names like *naturalmamaof12boys* would give terrifying accounts of what modern medicine had done to women and our natural rhythms. How our bodies are perfect vessels, made for childbirth, and that interrupting the natural birth cycle with drugs would cause delays and stress to us and the baby. Or, in some extreme cases, we'd birth crackhead epidural babies. Worst-case scenario, they'd come out looking like Steve Buscemi, the googly-eyed actor in *Fargo*.

I would go into my doctor's office with a stack of printed-out blog posts, licking my finger and going one by one, daring my doctor to prove these women wrong. It didn't matter how many times she told me epidurals were perfectly safe, I couldn't help but wonder if I might be an exception.

"No, epidurals do not cause your baby to get Steve Buscemi eyes, and that's a really inappropriate nonmedical term they're using," she said, snapping off her gloves. "But the blog post about the hemorrhoids is fairly accurate. Unfortunately, those can pop out during natural births, too, so who's to say?" Then she pulled up her stool and patted my hand. "Listen, I deliver many babies nearly every day, and most women opt for an epidural. It's perfectly safe but entirely up to you. This is your experience; follow what would make you most comfortable."

Sound advice, but what if nothing was currently making me comfortable? Not my underwire, not my acid reflux, not my bed, not the baby's butt in my lungs, and not any of the decisions I had to make about my birth process. This wasn't an ice cream parlor; it's not like I could try a sample of an epidural or natural childbirth and see which one felt right. Besides, I routinely regret my ice cream choice and spend the rest of the drive home begging my husband to swap.

I really did respect my doctor, even though I could tell she was a little put off by the "All Doctors Are in the Pocket of Big Pharma" blog post. I liked her a lot and tried to impress her. I'd crack jokes and drop hints about "books I'm writing," sort of hoping she'd invite me to lunch and we could just chat and bond and get to know each other. Pregnancy is such a scary and vulnerable time for any woman, and our doctors are like firemen rescuing us from a burning building. Naturally, something developed between me and my doctor that went beyond feelings. Soul mates, maybe? After all, she had been places even my husband hadn't been. If I couldn't trust her, *who could I trust*?

Despite this fondness, I still couldn't resist cheating on her with other hysterical mothers online. The internet made you think you were taking the red pill in *The Matrix*. Suddenly you saw the truth: that cool latex outfit you'd been wearing was actually a shabby knit sweater covered in moth holes. The drama in the forums, the anecdotal evidence, and the harrowing tale of the sister's friend's third cousin's botched hospital birth all had me on the edge of my seat. Like clockwork, I would find myself in bed, pulling out my iPhone. Its screen lit up the darkened room as my beady little eyes obsessively googled worst-case scenarios.

It also didn't help that my first pregnancy was in the height of the all-natural movement. Doctors weren't respected; they were put to the test. Did they know unrefined coconut oil could put out the unwieldy fires of a yeast infection? Didn't think so! We had to take matters into our own hands. You couldn't throw a dead cat without someone selling, rubbing, or misting essential oils. Women were naming their daughters "doTERRA" and "Eucalyptus" and swearing that a little lavender on your wrists prevented stretch marks and pregnancy-induced skin tags.

I remember the day Jen made a new friend at church who sold doTERRA and made her own kombucha. Jen would never be the same. Before I knew it, instead of making fun of our husbands like we used to, we were talking about the benefits of a paleo lifestyle. It was shortly after one of these conversations that she informed me she would be having a natural water birth at home, guided by her trusted midwife. All came highly recommended by Kombucha Jane.

I tried to be supportive and not ask questions like "Why?" with a disgusted look on my face. It was none of my business, really. I think a woman should do whatever she wants. It's her pregnancy, her birth, her business. But for me, I just felt like epidurals were God's way of finally throwing us a bone. Who was I to not accept this gift?

But as I lay there in the hospital bed like a blubbery dead seal, I started to wonder if I had gotten this all wrong. The truth is, I'm a bit all-natural myself. I eat Ezekiel 4:9 bread, and my eggs come from chickens that wander the plains freely, thank you very much. So was this too sterile? Too impersonal? Terribly unnatural? Had I asked for the epidural too soon? Should I have been more emotionally and physically connected to the rhythm of the birth process and more spiritually connected to the blinding, ripping pain of childbirth?

I processed all of these questions and felt a little glum. "You're having a contraction," my husband said sweetly. "Want me to spin your bed around so you can have a look at the monitor?"

The exercise ball blew out from my knees. "Oh, what's the use!" I wailed. "Just let me know when it's time to push." I was all up in my feelings. Was I pathetic? Would it be more powerful, more satisfying, to be in my own bedroom, moaning wildly and pushing this baby out like a grown woman—carpet stains be damned? I started to recall conversations I'd had with friends who'd had natural childbirths. I told one that I didn't think there was any way I would "choose" that kind of pain, and she stopped me, cocked her head, and said, "Why do you feel that way? You're so much stronger than you think. Believe in yourself." Although I don't think my friend intended to waft an air of superiority in my direction, my hair blew back nonetheless.

And excuse me, but I do believe in myself! Especially my ability to bypass unnecessary, unimaginable pain. I was getting all ruffled up just thinking about it. Instead of all of us trying to figure this out together and encouraging one another to make the best decisions for ourselves, it was obvious that epidural births were seen as the choice of weak women who risked the health of their babies for their own comfort, and natural births were for warrior women, selfless and superior in mind, body, and spirit. Or, depending on the forum, epidural births were for women who had a good sense of humor and rock-solid common sense, while natural births were for women who wore long denim skirts, smelled like hemp, and took things a bit too seriously.

Of course, no one fits into any of these boxes, but like cliques in high school, we just end up taking on the identity of the loudest and craziest among us. Still, I didn't want to just pick a side; I wanted to be informed. And could someone tell me if twilight sleep was available by request?

My mom was a hundred steps ahead of the natural movement before that was even a thing. Vegetables were from our organic garden, grains were ground on our kitchen island, and desserts were sweetened with just a touch of honey. She did make exceptions for holidays, though. One Fourth of July, I was allowed as much bottled Coca-Cola as I wanted. I took long, crisp swigs while watching my brother fire off bottle rockets toward the neighbor's roof. I felt like I could live forever.

In high school, while kids were getting talks about smoking and drugs, I would find pamphlets on my pillow about the dangers of aspartame. At the time, I was in full rebellion and had an all-encompassing addiction to forty-four-ounce Diet Pepsi fountain drinks, which I'd get daily at the Bucky's gas station. *Holistic* wasn't a four-letter word in my home, and in many ways, it's still a big part of who I am.

But my mom, my greatest inspiration, was actually more neutral on childbirth because she knew all options had their own pros and cons. She'd had my sister in the early '70s under twilight sleep and bottle-fed because no one informed her there were other options. The experience made her feel a bit sad and disconnected, but luckily, when it was time to have my brother, twilight sleep had gone out of fashion. She was still medicated for his birth but chose to breastfeed him, considered totally barbaric at the time. For me, she let the freak flag fly and went completely natural. Mind you, in the early '80s, this was not a thing. As the story goes, Mom screamed so loudly during my birth, my dad tried to slip out of the room. As he hit the door, a nurse snatched the neck of his shirt, got an inch from his face, and growled, "You're not leaving before you make her take something, Mr. Lind."

"I can't make her do anything!" my dad shouted, and he pushed his way out of the room. I think he cried, but no one in my family will confirm.

My older sister never intended to have a natural birth, but her middle son came too quickly. When the nurse said it was too late for an epidural, she grabbed the collar of her husband's polo and let the spittle fly in his face. "Find someone who will give me an epidural, now!" She proceeded to rip his shirt nearly in half, like Hulk Hogan, popping off five fake nails in the process. When I visited her later, she looked right at me with her bloodshot eyes and said coldly, "Listen to me; I'm your older sister. Don't ever have a natural birth. Ever."

Okay, fine, hers was bad, but what's up with all these women singing its praises? They admit it hurts, but in a spiritual way, like fasting or posing with your ankles behind your head. They had their babies on beds of rose petals. It was fast and miraculous. They allowed photographers in the room to capture each moment and have large black and whites of themselves naked, groaning on all fours. They've hung the photos above their fireplaces. I mean, what gives?

After Jen had her kombucha-inspired home birth, I wanted

every single detail. She recounted her birth story candidly and was patient through all my questions. Was she really buck naked in the tub in front of everyone, and did she know what to do with her hands? Or boobs? Did she ask permission from her landlord? Did she have her house cleaned, the floors vacuumed? I felt like clutter and childbirth were a bad mix.

She spared no detail.

They had purchased an inflatable pool they set up in her bedroom. It was colorful, like a rainbow, with water features that needed to be blown up separately. Her husband filled it with air manually and partially fainted at least six times. They brought in a hose from the backyard to fill it up, in case you were wondering. Her midwife arrived and inspected the baby pool in the bedroom. "Right, so, this won't do. The sides will collapse," she said matter-of-factly.

"Oh, crap. What do we do now?" Jen asked.

"Your bathtub is an option, but it needs to be sanitized."

"Perfect!" Jen was desperate to make this work. "It's totally sanitized! I did all of that before you came," she said, overly enthusiastic. "Will you excuse me?" She ran into her bathroom, removed the shaver and hair clumps, then scrubbed the tub furiously before her midwife felt tempted to check on her.

Jen said it was fun and exciting in the beginning. She rolled around on an exercise ball, and despite the occasional contraction, she was in good spirits, cracking jokes and letting everyone know she couldn't wait to dig into her homemade granola after it was all over.

But things swiftly took a dark turn.

Her contractions escalated, and she was quickly moved into the tub. As her contractions increased, she started to get that wild look in her eyes. The same look people get when something real bad is about to happen and there's nothing they can do about it. At one point she announced that it had been a good run, but it was time to call it and make their way to a hospital, where they had things like epidurals.

"Oh, honey," her midwife said. "It's way too late for that."

Jen went into fight-or-flight mode. She started running furiously back and forth in the tub on her knees, creating a wild, splashy, whirlpool effect. She kept screaming, "I changed my mind! HELP ME, PLEASE!" But her midwife was right; it was too late. Soon, she gave birth to her son and felt every single bit of it.

"It was such a beautiful moment, Anna," she said blissfully over the phone.

"Sounds like it!" I said, laughing nervously.

"Really, when it's time for you to have kids, you should consider doing it at home. It's the way it's supposed to be—familiar, comfortable, surrounded by loved ones."

I cleared my throat. Now I was confused. Did she forget the entire first chapter of her birth story?

"I guess there's only one thing that's a little weird," she said, her voice trailing off.

"Oh? Weirder than you screaming and running around your bathtub on your knees?"

"My placenta's in the freezer."

Apparently, even the all-natural crowd can be guilted into not being natural enough, and her midwife's look of disappointment when she requested her placenta be discarded instead of made into a post-birth smoothie is why she eventually compromised to "save it for later." So there it sat, in the freezer, for years— like a horrific family secret, hidden underneath a bag of organic broccoli.

I guess recalling her candid story made me realize there's no real parenting utopia. Just options, pros and cons, preferences based on culture, personality, and whatever you can get your hands on at the time. Even though my friend loved giving birth at home and went on to do it two more times, her story was enough to give me peace that I had made the right decision, for myself, to have my baby in a hospital, paralyzed and pain-free. Where I didn't even have to see my placenta if I didn't want to, and no one would guilt me into making it into a smoothie or storing it in Tupperware in my freezer. Besides, Tupperware was expensive, and no amount of Method dish soap could make it right again.

I felt sensation in my body again, and that really perked me up. As I was able to move more freely, things felt less grim. At the same time, my contractions were escalating rapidly. At least that's what they told me. I had been turned over to my other side and was engulfed in another episode of *Rehab Addict*. They paged my doctor, and with a little help, I rolled onto my back. I was about to have a baby girl, and I had already named her Lucy. Despite spending most of my twenties wondering if I even wanted to be a parent, I guess I did want to be highly inconvenienced for most of my good years after all.

I got into position, feet in stirrups, ready for anything—except for pooping all over my doctor. *Dear Lord, don't let me poop*, I prayed. In retrospect, I should have prayed for a safe delivery, but I just couldn't get my mind off more important things, like crapping in front of a room of medical professionals. Also, my thighs came top of mind again as they flipped back into plain view. But it was my time to shine, so I made the decision to simply focus on the task at hand. Out of nowhere, a young, fresh nurse opened up a cabinet and pulled out a large mirror. "Would you like to watch?" she asked innocently.

I smiled, faintly. "Get that mirror away from my vagina or I'll burn this hospital down to the ground." Her eyes grew wide, and she rolled it back in the closet, slammed the door, and scuttled off.

Soon after, I had a baby. I immediately noticed her eyes were green, just like her daddy's. And she looked nothing like Steve Buscemi.

ELEVEN

UNFOLLOWED

Wrapped in a hospital gown, holding Lucy, I did what came naturally to me as a new mother—I checked my Facebook notifications. It was getting late, and the cafeteria was closed, so Rob left to get us some takeout at my favorite brewery, Lazlo's. I ordered ribs and onion rings, with a side of their creamy garlic sauce. I didn't bother to consider the logistics of eating baby back ribs in a hospital bed while holding a newborn baby.

Statistically speaking, newborns are a guaranteed social media home run, so I was eager to see how my post was performing. I had just posted a picture of Lucy right after she was born because babies don't exist unless their births have been announced on Facebook. Even the girl I hadn't spoken to since meeting at a book club six years ago had slapped a heart on it, and it was all very satisfying.

I find post-birth photos are the one time we'll allow the worst picture of our lives to get shared on social media. Our hair is slicked with sweat in a frizzy high bun. Our drooping, makeupless faces are trying to conjure a blissful smile. Or, if we had time in between contractions to put a face on before hopping in the car, our mascara is now smeared all over our eyes like a raccoon. I don't know why, but the hospital gown is always off one shoulder, and that shoulder looks bizarrely undefined and untanned, like a soft, white down pillow. But we allow it because our battle-weary appearance is a source of immense pride. There are exceptions, of course. Some women look like they just won a beauty pageant in their post-birth photos, which begs the question—*Why?*

As I scrolled through my likes, my mind wandered to the business partner I'd had a falling-out with, whom I'll call Bubbles. She was in my life during two of my miscarriages, so I thought she'd find Lucy's birth significant. She had done some work for me, and in her heart she was a good person, but she was a bit of a pathological liar. She was the type that would walk into a room and tell you she's a quadriplegic, then get super ticked if you asked an obvious question like, "So, how are you walking?" Truthfully, I admired that kind of boldness, but I obviously couldn't trust her, so things got dicey. The trouble was, we had mutual friends she had introduced me to, so as she undoubtedly gave them her fictional version of events, I sensed they were all souring on me. It wasn't obvious, of course. It's not like they were a prison gang, circling all around me with shanks. They didn't unfriend me right away—that seemed too emotional, too publicly petty. No, no. They went the more sophisticated, passive-aggressive form of adult revenge—the Unfollow. I think that's what they did, anyway. I don't really know, but I'm pretty sure. All I know is they stopped "liking" my posts, even the ones that only the devil himself could ignore, like photos of my freshly squeezed newborn baby. I was rubbed raw.

As I held my darling Lucy close to my chest and scrolled one-handed with my thumb, I noticed Bubbles hadn't liked the photo because she had probably, audaciously, unfollowed me. I decided to check her profile directly because obviously I had unfollowed her ages ago. As I typed in her name, I was unable to see her entire profile. I was confused until it hit me—*That little tramp unfriended me.* Me! Wow. I mean, WOW. I spat in disgust. If anyone should have been unfriending, it was me. I typed in the names of our mutual friends and *bam*. All had unfriended me. Me! What kind of sick world was I living in?

I shifted in my hospital bed, trying to manage gurgling, angry waves splashing in the pit of my stomach. It was the kind of sensation you get when someone pulls out in front of you and then lays on their horn as if *you* were the problem. It's such a pure injustice that one can't recover easily.

My mind trailed off to a year prior, when I was having lunch with my close friends Brady and Amber. We were reminiscing about an old friend and coworker we hadn't seen in years. I brought up her Facebook marriage announcement, casually, while heading back to our charcuterie board. Puzzled, Brady said, "Oh really? I didn't see her post anything about getting married." He pulled up his phone and, with eyes wide and jaw firm, spat, "That little tramp unfriended me." Amber and I laughed and laughed and laughed, only to take momentary breaks to sip our wine, then laugh and laugh and laugh again. But Brady didn't think it was funny. Sure, he pretended to laugh it off—but the way he halfheartedly engaged in our funny banter for the remainder of the afternoon told me a different story.

"The underwire in my new swimsuit is a fraud," I said, popping a piece of cheese in my mouth. "Keep it real; it's a saggy-boob suit. Grown women aren't swimming; we're trying to get a little sun while yelling at our kids to stop splashing because they're getting our hair wet." Brady offered a courtesy laugh.

"So funny," he said, lips pressed flat, eyes distant and off-center.

It was obvious he couldn't get his mind off his recent slap in the face. To help him manage, we threw out a possible timeline of the unfriending. "What's the last thing you remember her posting?" we pressed.

"I don't know. I think it was a selfie with that guy she was dating, the one with no neck?" he offered. Amber and I stole glances.

"Oh dear, that was about three boyfriends ago." We shifted focus and threw out possible explanations for what could have caused it.

"I know!" I said, slapping the table. "I bet it was when you were posting updates every ten minutes for that 'Free Health Care for Strippers Bowl-a-Thon' you participated in."

"What's wrong with free health care for strippers? Don't they deserve the dignity of medical care?"

"Well, yeah, of course," I said, tiptoeing forward with caution. "It was just like—you just posted every single donation. Some people, you know, um, have a low threshold for that is all, um . . . is all I'm saying." Brady shot back his wine and poured another. We reassured him that philanthropic status updates, however frequent, were not worthy of an unfriending and concluded that it was most definitely some Facebook glitch, the excuse we all make when passive-aggressively rejected on social media. But for the rest of the evening, you could tell he wasn't comfortable. How could he be, with all those gurgling, angry waves splashing around?

Full of self-pity in my hospital bed, I was fully aware I was reaching a new emotional low. I had just given birth to my first-born, and there I was, circling the toilet of gross insecurities. I forced myself to pretend it didn't bother me as a welcome distraction entered my room, carrying huge bags filled with ribs. Rob laid out my meal on my little pullout table before reaching out his arms to take Lucy and put her in the bassinet. I refused the gesture. I'm not sure why I was so adamant on holding her at all costs, but I think it's because I had waited so long to have my sweet baby, it was going to take more than a few slippery baby backs to let her go. I ate my ribs one-handed and sloppy, like a cave woman. Every so often I'd dip an onion ring into the thick garlic sauce that would drip four to eight times all over us on its way to my mouth. It was a beautiful foreshadowing of the crumbs, guacamole, salsa, cheese dip, and leftover mongolian beef that would fall on Lucy's sleeping head and body in the many months to come.

The meal hit all the right spots, but I wondered if the garlic sauce might have been a bit offensive by the way the nurse came in and then blew back as if struck by a gust of wind. Rob, stuffed and satisfied, sized up the stiff, miserable couch that was to be his bed for the evening. It seemed silly for him to stay, as I had more help than I could possibly need with a kind and attentive staff. "There's no reason you should be miserable tonight," I told him. "Go home and come back to us in the morning." After much protesting, Rob relented, kissed his girls goodbye, and left us in a dimly lit room. I found myself alone again with our daughter and my hormones. I felt confused and aggressive, like a soldier elated to have won a battle but now facing new, urgent orders. Brimming with joy, I was prepared to destroy my enemies and then weep for no reason and all reasons, for a long, long while. Exhausted, but too wired to sleep, I dialed up my mom and gave her the latest updates in excruciating detail (I found a fun-sized Snickers in my bedside table!), dancing around what I really wanted to talk about. "So, I know this is random," I began, "but you remember that girl who used to work for me? The one Whole Foods Linda had a sense about? I just found out she unfriended me, and all of our mutual friends unfriended me too."

"Okay," she said. "So?"

"So"—my voice cracked—"it hurts my feelings!" I whimpered quietly into the phone while dipping a cold onion ring into garlic sauce.

"Oh good grief!" she snapped. "Who cares!"

"I do, I guess," I said, taking a napkin to Lucy's head.

"Anna, honey, do you really? Truly, who cares? Why are you letting this bother you now?"

"I don't know," I sniffled. Her blunt reaction, believe it or not, was making me feel better. I love when someone blows off my deepest fears; I really do. I don't want to show a weird mole to my doctor and have him grip my shoulders and warn me I could be in for the battle of my life. I want him to wave it off and say something flippant like, "We'll test it, but it's nothing. Have you been outside today? It's gorgeous!" This is the approach I prefer from my friends and family. I don't want to be disrespected and ignored, but I like being reminded that it's not the end of the world until the world actually ends. It gives me permission to lighten up and enjoy life. As my mom lovingly yet firmly dissuaded me from indulging my impulse to focus on the exact opposite of what I should have been focusing on, I felt I could grab on to her sentiment and let it float me peacefully to sleep. "Maybe it's my hormones," I said with a yawn. "I just hate getting rejected, even by people I never liked in the first place."

"No one likes rejection, but some people won't like us no matter what we do, and the sooner you let these slights roll off you, the happier and freer you'll be," she said. "Now, it's been a long, wonderful day. Get some rest; things always look better in the morning."

We hung up right as Lucy began to fidget, fuss, and root. I leaned back, and we attempted to nurse, which was mostly awkward trial runs in the beginning. But we got into a rhythm, and I rode my oxytocin high into the ethers, letting my mind wander free. It meandered to a memory of about five months prior when I was on a nesting bender. I started going through all my closets, drawers, and cupboards, getting rid of anything I hadn't seen, noticed, or used within a year. This was long before Marie Kondo, so I wish I had trademarked my nesting bender organization system, but too late now. Decluttering was so freeing that I hit up Facebook to do the same. I went through every person in my Friends list and unfriended anyone who hadn't engaged with me in over a year. With a few quick taps, I unfriended almost a hundred people, including, of course, Bubbles and all our mutual friends.

Oh boy, that's embarrassing, I thought, brushing my cheek against the top of Lucy's head. Luckily, the only people privy to my most embarrassing thoughts and insecurities were the two people I could trust the most—my mom and a kid who couldn't talk.

When I read some of my favorite humor writers, the experience is a splash of cold hard truth right to the face. I imagine it's how the celebrated star soprano of a small-town church choir might feel if she sat right next to Celine Dion while the celebrity belted out "My Heart Will Go On."

"Oh," the soprano would say quietly to herself, "I see." Then, as Celine hit octaves that aren't actually humanly possible (*Probably because Celine has some kind of freak throat deformity*, the soprano would assure herself), the small-town star would slowly exit the stage, make her way to a large plot of land, and dig a hole in the ground big enough to lie in for a while.

One of life's most aggravating truths is that no matter how much we love to do a thing, and no matter how good we are at it, someone, somewhere is out there doing it better than we are. Or worse, they're far less talented and simply have better branding, resources, or connections. And have more followers on Instagram. And are the type that eats half a cookie and forgets to eat the other half. And they're the worst.

In the early days, when millions were first awakening to the idea that getting internet famous might be a solid life's purpose, the experts had you believe there were strict formulas for success. Post every day on your website, 4.3 times on Facebook, 2.8 times on Instagram, and 5,456.32 times on Twitter, for example. But I couldn't help but notice that the very best writers, the ones I admired most, never followed any formulas when it came to social media. They just posted whenever and didn't really seem to care much about the content. Some of them weren't even on social media at all. Still, many of the creatives I was meeting at conferences were finding success, getting famous, and livin' the dream, so it felt impossible to avoid the wave of endless possibilities. You could see the evolution of success with your own eyes—food blogger begins journey in her hometown of Wisconsin, in a modest home with a boring kitchen. A million followers later, and there she is, filming herself opening a FabFitFun box with enthusiasm in her new, all-white, high-gloss kitchen in LA. If she could do it, why couldn't I?

I needed the lowdown, so in the beginning I signed up for every blogging conference my credit card could handle. Sure, it was fun; I learned a lot and met cool people, but it reminded me of my first day of high school, except instead of worrying I'd get my period, I worried about getting a good ROI. My desire to succeed was fierce, activating the very worst parts of my temperament. It's probably how actors feel waiting to audition, looking around and sizing everyone up. Except I wasn't sizing up so much as stalking everyone on Facebook to see if they had more followers than I did. Was it so hard to just relax, enjoy, and learn? Apparently, because I was just foraging around, indulging my most primitive instincts. Jealous, competitive, but desperate to belong.

In New York at the Midtown Hilton, I was waiting in line to get coffee before Katie Couric's keynote when one of the very first, and most famous, mommy bloggers walked by on her way to the conference room. She was flanked by women, like some sort of posse. Her pace was brisk, and a few in her group were taking quick triple steps to keep up. *Just who does she think she is?* I thought. *Beyoncé?* I was both disgusted and super jealous. *I wanna be in a posse!*

I found a spot at a table up front, perfectly positioned for Katie and me to make lots of eye contact. We did, once, and despite our souls connecting for that fleeting moment, I still felt a sense of unease, as if I had walked into a room, looked around, and wondered, *Wait, why did I walk in here again?* As I took notes and introduced myself to people with too much enthusiasm between break-out sessions, I started to form a hypothesis. From what I could tell, I had two paths to success. One: I could follow my spirit. Know that I am worthy just as I am and write daily. Study, practice, and have faith that consistency and the good work of my hands would be blessed. Or, two: I could just try to get Facebook famous. I wasn't getting any younger, so I went with Facebook famous.

But getting famous on Facebook is no easy task—you don't just show up and post a bunch of stupid things online and get throngs of followers. Well, some people do. Okay, lots of people do, but they're still the exception, not the rule. I needed a plan. A formula. I love formulas because they give me the kind of false sense of certainty that helps me sleep at night. Straying from a formula to "try my own thing" or "get creative" was a risk I wasn't willing to take. It could take years off the clock, and I needed to be filming myself opening FabFitFun boxes, like, yesterday. Further, I didn't want to join the club I call "People Who Are the Worst." I'm not referring to murderous dictators or that ShamWow guy. Rather, I'm referring to people who don't follow the prescribed formula, then blame somebody else for their failures. Take, for instance, your favorite Ina Garten recipe. Go through her thousands of reviews, and you'll find more than one bad reviewer who strayed from the formula, then blamed Ina for it. The review goes something like this:

MelissaLovestoBake81
★ **Do Better, Ina**

I'm sorry, I have to give these muffins one star—this just didn't work for me. They came out flat and firm like hockey pucks. Instead of all-purpose flour, I substituted almond, and instead of sugar, I used agave, and I was all out of baking powder, so I left it out. I usually love you, Ina, but this was a big flop! What a waste of good ingredients!

People who leave these kinds of reviews are truly the bottom of the barrel, and I'd rather die than be one of them. So I became a meticulous student, learning not just how many times to post but at what time of day to post. I researched how to create attractive headlines and eye-catching memes and what kind of posts outmaneuvered Facebook's algorithm (hint: none of them). I figured out how to make my website flow and keep people on it longer. Every trick, tool, method, and, most importantly, formula, was implemented to the best of my ability. It should come as no surprise that this was after I had gone viral with the fart story—when I was so new I didn't even realize there were formulas. I just wrote, easy, free, and happy, to no one in particular because no one knew I existed. But I was convinced that wasn't a real formula I could sink my teeth into; I had to labor endlessly and drain myself dry emotionally to succeed.

I didn't actually want to be famous, per se. It seemed like internet fame eventually led to an emotional breakdown, a divorce, or some kind of sex/drug/adopt-a-baby-from-China-then-return-it scandal. I just wanted, no, *I needed* to be successful. I had decided against using my master's degree in interpersonal communication for a job that cuts actual checks to chase a dream that was cutting zero checks and caused Rob and me to live on edge 24/7. Failing would break my heart. I had to make it work, and the only key to success I could see was that shiny, untouchable, miserable little social perk from my youth: popularity. I needed followers. Lots of them. On the internet, success follows the most follows. The currency is likes, comments, and shares. Little finger taps on a screen from strangers are now more precious than silver.

The more popular you are, the more opportunities, book deals, sponsorships, paid advertising, appearances, and speaking fees—plus better hair and thighs—you are likely to have. But have you ever tried to be popular? It's like trying to give yourself a nickname—it's a total disaster, and no one respects you afterward. I was in for a rough, awkward ride.

The formulas did work, a little, but they can only go so far. Formulas don't account for talent, and they don't account for providence. They don't consider the potholed road that leads us to who we were created to be. It's a boring, long road with lots of roadblocks that really get you peeved. You have to pull over to get gas, change flat tires, and sometimes hitch a ride in the back of someone's truck for a while. Every dream worth doing comes at a cost, and we have to train for it. The road is intended to be a pain in the butt—otherwise, how would we cope with the inevitable rejection? Bad review or shut door? The dreaded unfollows? Faith builds from experience, stamina through steep hills you'd rather avoid. Dreams are heavy; we have to be fit enough to carry them.

But that's boring, so I tried a few shortcuts. I fought fiercely for fast, temporary, fickle rewards, only to feel sorry for myself when my efforts didn't pan out. I'd never admit this out loud, but I measured my worth by how well my writing "performed." If something I wrote did well, I'd leap forward like a ballerina, spinning and twirling and leaping. If it didn't do well, my stomach would roll, and I'd snip and snap my mood all over the people who love me most. It's hard to imagine—worth dependent on a finger tap. A like, a heart, a follow from a stranger.

I forgot why I had walked into the room. Little Anna, the precious, chubby girl who carried all her tiny but profound hurts, would peek in from time to time. She pretended to hide, but I saw her, of course. I always do. She seemed disappointed things weren't much improved. *We're grown now,* I felt her saying. *Aren't we tired of caring about what all these people think?*

Yes, I was so tired. It began with God's seed of a dream, planted in my heart as a little girl, to one day become an author. I wanted to make people laugh, see themselves in my words, and have hope. Maybe I'd get a book published, do a few book signings, some readings too—why not? There were no pressures; there was no need for likes and man's approval. The desire, so innocent, childlike, and pure, was to simply become who I was made to be. It was such a delightful dream a little girl could dream, writing away in a Hello Kitty notebook in my room with the door closed.

For nearly a decade after my first viral story, nothing much happened. No growth, no big opportunities. Definitely no money. No fame. But failing to succeed in all the wrong things was the best thing to ever happen to me. Ten years was the exact length of time it took for me to stop giving one more single crap about what simply did not matter. The unfollows, the mean comments, the critiques about my hair. They just fell off, one by one, as I eventually realized how cheap they really were. The attention, once a shiny necklace, eventually turns your neck green. Ten years is a long time, I know. But the road is long, and it takes what it takes.

I never quit writing, but I finally quit chasing. I went back to the beginning. I tore up formulas and the perfect hashtags. I searched inside for what made me happy and contented. I scanned for what gave me direction and purpose. I focused on the craft, not the likes. I focused on making one person's day better, not one million. Be a light. Be myself. That's so easy to do, it's stupid. Why hadn't I thought of it before?

Two years after giving birth to Lucy, I gave birth to Poppy. The nurses tended to her, wrapped her tight, and put her into the bassinet while they helped me hoist up a pair of degrading mesh panties around my waist. Poppy slept soundly in her little hospital cap, and I couldn't help but take a picture of her and put it on Facebook. I lifted her from the bassinet, and as I held my brand-new, red-haired baby, I forgot to check the notifications. Mostly because I had misplaced my phone, but also because I didn't even care enough to look for it.

I delivered Poppy late in the evening, and Rob and I were starving. The only place open was a nearby Wendy's. I would have eaten a barrel of shriveled gas station hot dogs at that point, so that was fine by me. Rob took my order, and I sent him off aggressively, doling out threats to return swiftly with the right order or so help him God. While I waited, I had nothing left to do but gaze at Poppy's bright-red, spiky hair. She reminded me of a Little Critter. I kissed her until she pulled her face from me like the cat pulled away from Pepé Le Pew. Rob took my threats seriously and returned promptly. I felt the kind of relief someone in distress feels when they hear the ambulance pull into the driveway. Rob started chatting my ear off about how the drive-through microphone was malfunctioning as I unhinged my jaw like a python to take a massive bite of my spicy chicken sandwich. Naturally, I dripped special sauce on Poppy's sleepy little head. The more things change, the more they stay the same.

"Want me to take her?" Rob said, growing concerned as the drips picked up tempo.

"No, we're fine," I told him, wiping the sauce away with my napkin. This wasn't my first rodeo.

Babies seem helpless, but they're strong enough to flip your world upside down. They immediately put life in perspective, providing us with a new to-do list. The fluff you used to put high on the list before their arrival is now somewhere toward the end. Or you forget to put it on the list at all.

As my girls grew older, the day-to-day of motherhood released the pressure of popularity, and it just . . . fizzled away. I enjoyed a new, lighter pep in my step. So happy, so free, to simply live, without wondering if the moment was perfect for Instagram.

Motherhood didn't strip me from my writing ambitions; it simply changed the purpose of those ambitions. After I took care of the needs of my family, I'd go write. Mostly for me. Maybe someone else would like it, too, but that wasn't any of my business. God created me to do what I was finally doing. And it was good.

Besides, who knows? Maybe if I kept it up, one day I'd become a published author. A little girl can dream the most delightful dream.

TWELVE

BABY IS FINE, BUT I'M DEAD

L ucy was only two days old, a teeny nugget of a baby, scrunched and cocooned in her little car seat. I'd like to say the drive home from the hospital was peaceful, but it was perilous. Even though Rob assured me he was going well under the speed limit, my instincts told me otherwise. As he crept up to stop signs, I jammed my foot into the floorboard, screaming, "Watch out, WATCH OUT!" As he merged onto the highway at a menacing twenty-five miles per hour, I shouted, "Slow down before you kill us all, you idiot!" We were so deeply on edge and vulnerable transporting our precious cargo that it was as if we were the new guy tasked with transporting ten tons of Colombian cocaine for Pablo Escobar. But by the grace of God, we made it home.

As we walked through the front door as a family for the very first time, Rob put down the bags he had around his neck and carried in Lucy while she slept in her car seat. I waddled in behind him with a firm grip on my complimentary insulated water mug and a bag filled with mesh undies and pads the size of twin beds.

Mom had been waiting for us at our apartment, taking care of our dog and cooking us a meal. She welcomed us with big hugs, and joy hung in the air so thick you could wrap it around you like a shawl. But even in its warmth, I couldn't shake a swift and deep desire to weep.

Our beloved first baby, a spoiled English bulldog named Bruno, made his way over to greet us. He had never been away from me for one night, let alone two. He was moody, as if my two-day stay at the hospital were on par with animal abuse and neglect. He was born without much of a tail, and he swayed his butt so vigorously when we arrived that he could barely make it down the hall to greet us. He sniffed Lucy with a hint of malice before sneezing in her face. Sitting back on his haunches, he huffed. *Yeah, I don't think so*, he seemed to say. *Keep the receipt.* He trotted back down the hall with the sort of confidence one displays when they believe they've solved a problem.

Mom was in our kitchen, prepping dinner, and brought out fresh rolls to celebrate the fresh baby. Rob dove in as I tried desperately to bat away deep sobby cries fluttering around my head. My hormones were running hot, and I had no control over my face, which coiled into an ugly cry formation.

"Honey?" Mom asked, tilting her head.

"I just need a moment with Lucy," I said and took her sleeping, curled body out of the car seat and wrapped her tightly in my arms. She had a stork bite on her forehead, in between her eyes (she still does, actually) that reminded me of Harry Potter's lightning bolt. I kissed it. I took her to her room and sat in the new cozy chair I'd purchased just for us. I gazed at the sleeping, tiny body and wept, deeply. You wouldn't have been surprised to see a new mother crying as she gazed at her darling, but you might have wondered why this particular mother was in the throes of the sobby, heavy, snotty kind of cry that one does at a funeral or, worse, when you're the only one of your friends who doesn't have a date to prom. Was I sobbing because it was just more love than I could handle? Or was it because I'd never poop in peace again?

I honestly can't tell you. That probably means it was more of a hormonal letdown than some spiritual awakening, but the moment reminded me of a verse in the Bible after Jesus was born and everyone was fussing around Mary and her new baby. Angels, shepherds, trumpets, donkey manure, a dirt-caked manger, frankincense, and myrrh. That's a lot for a woman to take in. The Bible says Mary didn't join in the frenzy happening around her. Rather, she took a moment for herself to "treasure all these things in her heart and to ponder them" (Luke 2:19). While that's a beautiful verse, it leaves me wanting. I know instinctively that Mary's feelings were deeper, greater, and more possessing. But I think language fails because nothing intellectual can hold up to the gravity of the experience. I guess as I sobbed, I, too, was treasuring, setting aside each moment as a keepsake. Pondering its weight. Blowing my nose heartily into an overpriced spit-up rag adorned with Lucy's initials.

After some time, I returned to the kitchen with my baby, a pair of puffy eyes, and makeup noticeably absent.

"Sorry. I had to cry super hard," I said. My mom nodded with recognition.

"Is there butter for these rolls?"

The initial few days of bringing a baby home are typically bliss. As you rest and repair and eat whatever you want with a refreshing conviction that you've earned it, the baby tends to just sleep and eat and poop, providing everyone with a false sense of security that the following year will be met with ease. But I was no fool. Women in the comment threads and baby forums came to the rescue as they projected their own anxieties, fears, and stories of death and destruction. They boldly made their unprecedented claims while warning, "Do your research!" And that I did. It's a wonder the human race hasn't gone extinct because, according to the internet, death has to be fought off at every pass, karate chopped and high kicked around every corner.

I don't want to brag, but I'd trained for this moment. Thanks to a steady indoctrination of self-righteous mommy blogs, combined with ten months of fierce academic research conducted at Google University, I didn't feel confident necessarily, but I was vigilant—and paranoid. I had consumed every personal anecdote on Facebook that happened to "BrandonAndKim" Schneider's aunt's cousin's baby and memorized every possible killer of children from the beginning of time: detergents, cleaning supplies, pesticides, toys, nuts, walkers, spinach, mountain cliffs, stairs, ramps, car seats, tree limbs, sleepy grandmas, birds (don't get me started on their deadly baths), locusts, mattresses, cattle, all forms of transportation—and that wasn't even the half of it. How many evenings had I spent reading about the deadly effects of crib bumpers? The evils of blankets? The doom of unwashed pacifiers? And the absolute carnage of a stroller not pushed to manual specifications? Enough to make your blood run cold.

One evening, while enjoying cheesecake with the post-pregnancy sense of entitlement, I knew there was only one possible outcome. I had read every heart-wrenching story of babies who'd died alone in their cribs due to their mothers' callous separation and babies who'd died next to their moms in bed because they were callously smothered. There was only one solution:

Mothers never sleep.

Not the good ones anyway.

At the end of my life, experts will find I spent eleven years watching Netflix, twenty-six years sleeping, ten waiting in line, and thirty-two reading reviews on Amazon. Eighteen of those will have been focused on reviews of lifesaving baby gadgets.

At my baby shower, one of my mom's friends gave me a baby monitor, but the old-school kind with no camera. How could I monitor her breathing obsessively throughout the night with this? I smiled graciously, but inwardly I scoffed. *SIDS has no sound!* I returned it, and I sprung for a top-of-the-line baby monitoring video system, complete with responsive phone app. Whatever hopes, dreams, sense of self, or ambitions I had before this child were now gone, replaced by a truer, nobler mission: monitor Lucy's breathing patterns at all times.

I won't sugarcoat it: my mission proved trying. Especially

because babies tend to breathe softly, normally, in an un-exaggerated way, making it easy for a mother on the brink to think she's seeing things, or worse, nothing at all. At night, I'd pull up video on my phone, looking for the slightest variation of night vision pixilation over her stomach. If I saw the pixels move a bit, I could deduce breathing was taking place. If not, SIDS. "Rob, does it look like she's breathing to you?" I'd ask him. At no response, I'd look over and see my sweet groom resting peace-fully, breathing deeply. That man had alotta nerve.

"Hey—Rob! ROOOOB!" I'd shout.

"What? WHAAAAAAT?!" he'd yell, leaping from bed, arms punching, heart racing.

"Does Lucy look like she's breathing to you?"

Eventually it became obvious I would need better monitor-ing, and perhaps security guards. But we were on an extremely tight budget, and I'd need to get creative by applying for new credit cards. Fortunately, Facebook easily deduced I was a new mother and relentlessly placed an ad in my feed for this device you clip on the baby's foot. It would monitor the baby's vitals and sound an alarm if something was amiss. But this type of peace don't come cheap. "So, um," I said, cozying up next to Rob on the couch, "you know how I've been trying to stay awake so I can monitor Lucy's breathing?"

"Mm-hmm," Rob said in that tone he has when he has con-cerns about where this is going.

"Well," I began, gently touching his hand, "there's this wonderful device that you hook to your baby's foot that moni-tors their vitals. The reviews are fantastic. All the mothers say it gives them great peace of mind. And that's what I need." I stared directly into his eyes. "*Peace of mind.*"

"So, our baby will go to bed hooked up to monitors like she's in the ICU?"

"Well, no. Of course not. A little." I giggled nervously, running my fingers over his forearm. "You're a nurse; you'd know better than me."

"How much does it cost?" he asked.

"Two hundred and fifty dollars."

"Two hundred and fifty dollars! Babe, no way. We don't have the money to spend on crazy devices that aren't necessary. She's healthy, she's safe, and we have a video monitor. We have to stop worrying like this." I immediately withdrew my affection. First of all, "we"? He slept, hard, all night long, like a drunken mouse. He wasn't worried about anything. *What do you mean, "we"?*

But now I was at an impasse. There was no way I was giving up, but the monitor was actually $500 and I'd started low with $250 to gently ease him into the shock, like a live lobster in a stockpot. I pulled up my laptop and got to work on a solution. About five hours later, I found myself knee-deep in the reviews for another monitor that was like a twelve-by-twelve-inch square you place under the baby's crib mattress. It was very sensitive, even to gentle breaths, and if it sensed no motion after ten seconds, a piercing alarm would sound. This, was, coincidentally, $250. Yes, this was a quandary, but perhaps if I came clean about the first monitor's price, I would have leverage to negotiate. I sauntered into the family room, where Rob was still on the couch, watching football.

"So, you'll think this is funny," I said, cuddling close.

"Mm-hmm," Rob said.

"I was wrong. The ICU monitor is five hundred dollars."

Rob blew up from the couch as if he were sitting on a geyser. "Five hundred dollars! We can't afford that!"

"All right, all right, all right!" I said, tugging his pant leg and gently bringing him down from the ceiling. "I agree, it's too much, and we can't afford it. I found another one that's much more affordable."

"How much?" he asked.

"Two hundred and fifty dollars." I braced, but Rob just sighed and took deep gulps of his Coke Zero.

"Really, babe," I continued, "I know it seems crazy to spend money like this when we have so little, but I'm a new mom, and every single thought in my mind centers on her safety." While gently rubbing his earlobe, I added, "It would help me be at peace while I sleep, and I'm just so exhausted." My lip started to quiver. *Wowza, I really need a nap.* "I mean, look at my boobs! They're giant, sore blimps! My nipples are blistered! I haven't showered in days, and my hair is matted in the back like a neglected shih tzu!" Rob softened as I kept rolling, like a snowball down a hill. "I'm the fattest I've ever been, I'm still wearing maternity clothes *that I hate*, and I can't fit into regular bras. I'm a mess! I'm just a mess," I said through sobs. Rob handed me a leftover Chipotle napkin to wipe the snot from my nose, but I wasn't finished. "And I need to sleep! I'm delirious and weepy and hormonal and *exhausted*. But I can't sleep because I worry every minute about her. I just need something to help me know she's okay while I sleep at night." I leaned into my cries, slumping into the couch, and boo-hooed.

"Okay, it's all right. I know this is hard," Rob said, rubbing my back. "Yes, if it will make you feel better, let's get it."

I perked up. "You mean it?"

"Yes, I mean it. Go ahead and get it."

"Great. Tracking says it will be here tomorrow by 3:00 p.m."

AnnaWithTheSoreNips
★★ Baby Is Fine, but I'm Dead
Reviewed in the United States, December 2014

I don't usually write a review, but I feel compelled to now that I have died and am corresponding from the afterlife. The alarm is so piercing and violent, my spirit simply exited my body without warning. We're pretty broke over here, so we didn't take this purchase lightly. The motion monitor itself works fine IF the baby sleeps directly over it, all night long. If your baby moves or rolls in their crib, then brace yourself to be awoken at 3:20 a.m. with the most horrific, shrill sound that can only be described as Lucifer's fire alarm. Also, if you get the baby in the morning and forget to turn the monitor off, please realize that when it no longer senses your baby, it will startle you so fiercely, you'll throw your baby across the room as a reflex. TWO STARS!

I awoke to a loud thump. The first moments you wake up to a sound feel peculiar because you aren't completely convinced you didn't dream it. I found myself in Lucy's room. I would like to tell you that I returned the Paranoid SIDS Motion Monitor and came to my senses, but I'm afraid I kept it. Even after leaving my scathing review, I still felt I couldn't have ultimate peace that Lucy was safe without it.

Speaking of Lucy, where was she?

At around four in the morning, she had cried out, hungry. I crawled into her room like a drunken college student who had discovered a low center of gravity made forward movement easier. When I got to her crib, I unhooked, untethered, disarmed, and pulleyed the various lifesaving devices I had purchased. Last but not least, I turned off the motion sensor. Terrify me with Lucifer's alarm once, shame on you. Terrify me with Lucifer's alarm twice, *shame on me.*

I had carried her to the rocker and nursed her peacefully, but that was the last thing I remembered. I heard strange sounds, like faint fussing and whimpering. I looked down and Lucy was at my feet. *On the wood floor.*

I DROPPED MY BABY, EVERYBODY.

I swooped her into my arms, checking every finger and toe. I kissed and soothed and cried. Rob was working the night shift, so I called my mom.

"Hello?" she answered, groggy but concerned.

"Mom!" I wailed. "It's Lucy!"

"What!" She was alert now. "What about Lucy, Anna, what?"

"I fell asleep nursing her and she fell off my lap!"

"Is she okay? Is anything hurt?"

"No, she's—she's fiiiiiine!" I heaved and sobbed.

"Oh, good grief, Anna. You're not the first mom to fall asleep and have their baby fall off the chair or bed or couch, and you won't be the last. I put you on the bed while I folded laundry, and you fell right off while I was standing there! And look: you're here now. Just fine."

"But she could have died!" I protested.

"Says who?"

"Says people on the internet!"

"Anna, listen to me. You ready? You listening?"

"Yes." *sniffle* *sniffle*

"Get. Off. The. Internet."

"But—"

"GET. OFF. THE. INTERNET."

"Okay."

"Okay. She's fine. Go back to bed."

We hung up, and I looked down at Lucy. *Oh no. Oh no!* She wasn't injured; it was worse. She was wide-awake, giggly, and kicking her feet real frisky, and it was still the wee hours of the morning. I, on the other hand, felt as if I had been drugged. My speech was slightly slurred, and I was experiencing an oddly deficient use of my right hip. I placed her on a blanket on the floor and surrendered to the fact we were up for the day. I'd just started the coffee when my phone rang.

"Hey!" Rob said, breathless. "I've been texting you. I just checked the monitor, and it looks tipped over or something. Is she okay? Do you have her?"

"What? Yes, she's right here. It's fine."

"Oh, phew. It scared me. Having the camera like that

made me think the place was ransacked." During the process of "unhooking" Lucy, I must have knocked it over. *What a worrywart!*

"Okay, geesh," I said, filling the coffee maker's canister with water. "She's with her mom, safe and sound. Where else would she be?" I'm not proud of it, but I was getting cocky. It's a little something I do when I've experienced one of my fears and realized it's not as serious as I thought.

As Lucy gummed on a soft toy, I made my way into her room and took the motion sensor out from under her mattress. It was making life scarier, not safer, and I was exhausted by fear and was now willing to move into new emotions, like worrying I had mastitis. I put the camera upright and blew Rob a kiss.

Before leaving her room, I stuffed my milk pads in my nursing bra with the same resolve a knight would feel putting on his armor. I knew it was just the beginning of my battle against fear while raising my baby. I'd fear stairs. I'd fear pools. I'd fear YouTube, Snapchat, and JoJo Siwa's inevitable "I'm not a kid anymore" sexy album. I'd fear high fevers, nice boys, mean girls, her driver's license, and college. It's a fine line between keeping your child safe and letting your fear steal their independence. I'd find a middle ground, somehow—my own mental health depended on it. I wanted to enjoy the moment, not fear the future. And in that moment, it was time for Lucy to nurse.

"I like your boob pads," Rob said through the speaker of the monitor.

"Oh, these old things?" I said, sashaying across the room.

"Where's Lucy?" he asked.

"Good question." I looked around the room and tried to remember where I'd put her. It was fine. Everything was fine, no need to panic. "Well, anyway," I said, bending down to unplug the camera. "I'm sure she's around here somewhere."

THIRTEEN

FEAR BOX

I scribbled down every thought on a three-by-five-inch index card. I didn't care how stupid it was or that my family might find it after my death and bear not just grief, but mild judgment. If I felt it true, I wrote it down. I filled up every corner, every crevice, front and back, before moving on to another card, filling that one up too. I had no idea I was such a fearful person until I saw all my fears scrunched and scrawled and scribbled in between. In fact, I tend to think I'm more aloof, like my dad, who brushes everything off as easy and solvable. "Worst-case scenario, you get to ride around on a knee scooter for a year," he told me casually on the phone when I was awaiting X-ray results from a bad fall. "What's the big deal?"

As annoying as that is, he's always had a point. I don't walk miles to fill buckets with toxic river water for my family like some women in third world countries do. I don't feel as if I should birth ten children because most of them will die before the age of five due to some horrific, and now preventable, disease. Bombs aren't dropping in my neighborhood as I flee with my babies in my arms. And if I did have to flee, at least I have legs to flee on. There was an *Oprah* episode I've never forgotten, highlighting a mother who lost both her arms and legs due to a flesh-eating bacteria. They showed clips of her at home, zipping around on an office chair, somehow managing to fix breakfast for her kids with all her nubs. She told Oprah that when her doctor said they'd have to amputate all her limbs to save her life, her response was, "Go ahead and get it over with so I can get back to my kids." My point is: 99.9 percent of the complaints that come out of my mouth on any given day are preeeeetty weak.

Even so, compared to some of my uptight friends who only let their children play in the front yard if they're on a leash, I thought I was doing pretty well for myself in the fear department. But after taking a good hard look at my list, I wasn't so sure. I was afraid of a lot of things. I scribbled down each fear that lingered behind my ears, relaxed behind my eyeballs, and set up camp in my gut, flooding my index cards in a frenzy until every fear was given its own place.

I wrote in a frenzy because *I* was in a frenzy. I had just received a text that Rob and I had less than a month to leave our lake home. It was a beautiful house on a cozy little lake, filled with a hodgepodge of old cabins, modest homes, and more stately ones too. We had a river in the front of the house and a lake in the back, our backyard a nice sandy beach. We had moved in with our two baby girls, and it gave me such a gentle peace that we were finally settled into our forever home. The only downsides were our slow country internet that brought me to my knees on a daily basis and our inability to qualify for flood insurance. (I guess the only homes that qualify for flood insurance are homes that don't actually flood.) Other than that, our living situation was just about perfect—a dream, really. A dream that a simple text message shook awake.

I barely had time to grieve our home because I didn't know where we would go in such a short amount of time. It was a crazy-hot seller's market, with boring box houses along train tracks getting ten offers each. And on top of it, our budget was maxed. Just the expense of boxes and packing tape had my lower lip trembling. Add caring for two small babies while packing up and out of my beloved home, and I felt like a squashed spider, wrapped up in toilet paper, swooshing around the bowl, wondering how things had gone south so fast.

My dad had built the house, but he built it for an investor. She had gone in with another builder, who walked away from the job halfway through with all her money, leaving her upside down by the time she hired my dad to finish the home. Still, even though someone else owned it, it was a signature Dick Lind home, which made it feel familial, special, and mine. I saw my dad in the quality of the woodwork, the craftsmanship of cabinets, down to our baseboards. Rob was still in school to become a nurse practitioner, and we couldn't afford the house, not even close. But in the year after Lucy's birth, I'd been eager to leave our small downtown apartment and felt like I couldn't bear living there for one more minute. But I couldn't find anything better that we could afford, so I felt stuck and suffocated living there, like the air was thick and spoiled. It's fascinating how a baby changes you so quickly. For one, I developed a new, insatiable desire for a lawn, as if I couldn't properly care for my child without diapers, a high chair, and grass. For two, I popped Lucy out and instantly transformed into a danger-seeking robot. I could detect someone high on meth within a two-block radius, and let me tell you, if I caught one whiff of crazy, I'd turn that stroller around and haul ass back to my apartment in a New York minute. Try me, meth heads. I dare you!

So it was, with a full and hopeful heart, I asked the owner if she would consider going into a rent-to-own contract with us, agreeing to negotiate the purchase of the home after Rob's graduation. It was a long shot, but her inability to sell the home without taking a loss gave me a sliver of hope. She agreed almost immediately. Her terms were generous, I was deeply grateful, and it felt as if life with our two babies was ready to begin. A fairy tale, with bad internet, but a fairy tale nonetheless.

Unfortunately, though, I'm a skimmer. Even with important documents, like contracts. As an overexplainer who can't help but write indulgent short stories in texts and emails, you'd think I'd have more compassion and patience for others who do the same. But, hypocritically, if what you've sent me is more than two paragraphs, I'll skim so fast it'll be like you never wrote the email in the first place. About a year ago, I was doing some work for someone who wrote me a thesis. The beginning of her email was so complimentary and airy, I dove right into skim mode and missed the "have to regretfully part ways" part and responded with, "Sounds good! I'll get you something by the end of the week!" That mishap was so paralyzingly awkward, I had to unfriend her on Facebook and deny she ever existed just to mentally get through it. You'd think I would have learned my lesson, yet I still skimmed the part of our lease that stated we would have to formally extend our contract by a particular date if Rob had not yet graduated. Without warning, one day after the missed deadline, the homeowner took advantage of the clause as the market went bananas and left a sharp text saying we had to either make an offer on the house by end of day or be out by the end of the month.

I'm not the type to interrupt your tears over a mean boss and say, "I'm sorry, but every two minutes, someone is diagnosed with cancer. Within that lens, can you get over it, please?" So I also don't judge myself for how I threw myself over my bed like Scarlett O'Hara and wept. Or for calling my mom and wailing and snotting for so long that she had to put me on speaker to finish the dishes. A dam burst wide open, and every insult, slight, bad break, and lingering hemorrhoid served as proof that I had been victimized my entire life. We would have to move into a dilapidated apartment; I'd have to give up my writing, podcast, and ministry for a more stable, full-time, miserable job; and all I had hoped for, worked for, sacrificed for—was gone. Just. Like. That.

"Well, that's a pretty bleak analysis," my mom said distantly, still on speaker, clanging around like she was the dishwasher at an Outback Steakhouse.

There are many aspects of my temperament that don't serve

me well, but I have one inherent trait that's bailed me out of emotional carnage more times than I can count. And that is an extremely low tolerance for self-imposed emotional suffering. Sure, I can lose it just like the next person, but when I've found myself reeling from a major disappointment or crisis, I can't tolerate the pain for long. I have to recover and fight and claw for hope, so I'll do anything I can to overcome the feelings of helplessness and victimhood. Especially when I've been the victim of my own mistakes. As I sat at my desk, begging for guidance on what to do and where to go, I felt an impulse to release every single fear onto a piece of paper. I needed to spill it out as a way of surrender, a way of saying to God, "Here, you deal with it. I've gotta feed the girls breakfast." I opened my desk drawer, found three-by-five index cards, and let it pour until there was no fear left undetected inside me. Then I slipped the cards into a wooden box on the shelf and promptly forgot all about it.

I was still nervous, but now my fears were located in a box, making room for faith and hope. Within the following couple of weeks, our real estate agent showed us as many houses as she could in our price range. In between showings, Rob and I would look at apartments to rent. You might think it would be rather easy to find a pet-friendly apartment for a family of four, but we somehow ended up on waiting lists or touring spaces with carpet someone had definitely died on alone. Others had shockingly little storage space or simply smelled like dirt and onions. I was deflating at a rapid pace. The competition to buy homes was so fierce that we started putting in offers for homes I didn't even like. There was one that was such an outrageous DIY nightmare;

the havoc this couple brought to the home with their poorly followed YouTube tutorials left its mark on me. And yet, even the house that appeared to be a child's craft project sold to someone else before we even left the driveway. One by one, the houses tipped well above their worth to the highest bidder. Vibrating from nerves, I went for a walk so I could have a good chat with God alone.

I get why some people don't believe in God. They probably feel about me the same way I feel about Scientologists. Nothing, and I mean nothing, could come between me and my unbridled passion for *Top Gun* Tom Cruise. Until, of course, I watched a Scientology documentary. Then I walked backward, slowly, out of the room, terrified people actually believe in that crap.

Believing in God is a little silly, if you think about it. Almost embarrassing. But then again, to me, it also feels silly to believe that perfect order came from chaos. Or that the earth's axis is so frightfully perfect, the slightest variance left or right would kill us all. Or that our DNA is an actual instruction manual for our cells. I just can't help but wonder—who wrote the manual? I agree with my atheist friends: believing in God is like believing in magic. But have you ever studied the human eye? That's all the magic I need to believe. I like to keep it simple.

I've always felt connected to God, in a very precious and childlike way. I don't get weird about it. I just know that despite all my failings and frequent mistakes, I'm still loved, taken care of, sought after, and tended to. I've never been immune to consequences, but when I miss the train, magically a new one has always arrived, never early but always on time. It's only when I take it all for granted, or boot the train engineer off the train, that things start to inevitably go off the rails.

A few weeks ago, I planned to gift Lucy a new Barbie. She had played all her current Barbies ragged, and I felt like treating her to one after an early dismissal from school. When I told her we were on our way to Target to get a new Barbie, she bounced and rattled like she was on a wooden roller coaster. But once we arrived and started perusing the aisles, I noticed a growing sense of entitlement bubbling up and out her lips. Barbie, once worth several Liza Minnelli high kicks on the way into Target, was now a toy for peasants, apparently. She wanted a gift more on her level, like a two-hundred-dollar bike that she couldn't even ride. After I shut that down, she floated leaving Target altogether to go buy an actual live horse. Her wants for more expensive toys evolved into full-out demands, and it didn't take long to naughty her way into no gift at all. As I gripped her hand, she screamed all the way to the car, crying loudly all the way home, as tears of entitlement turned into pitiful tears of regret. But alas, she is my beloved, and Lucy, who had missed her train, got to hop on another one in due time.

I can't blame her, really. Tantrums are a human condition. I throw entitled fits nearly every day (mostly internally, as I wish to preserve my social standing). And yet, I feel so unconditionally loved by the Creator of the universe that I believe I'll always get that second chance. Another train will eventually *toot-toot* and let me aboard.

My walk picked up steam, and I felt an intense desire to take full responsibility. The raw truth was, I was in a mess of my own making. Years prior, Rob had lovingly and confidently agreed that after leaving my job at the university, I could take time to pursue a writing career. That was when he was in school to become a nurse and our income was abysmal, but I wanted it so bad that we made it work. The trouble was, I didn't want to live like a starving artist with a nursing student husband. I wanted to live like an Oprah's Book Club author with a doctor husband. We leased small but cool downtown apartments we could barely afford and accrued massive debt in the process. Rob eventually worked nights, with long, grueling hours, to help us meet a basic budget, and our relationship took a lot of bloody hits and blows. After we experienced a miscarriage during a gap in insurance, we went through a financial free fall that led to shame and denial. We had one foot set precariously on a banana peel with no relief in sight.

As much as I wanted to blame the homeowner for callously kicking us out of my home, the truth was—it was never mine. We weren't ready. We hadn't earned it. In my heart, I knew one day I'd make it as a writer, and I'd finally have a career to help us. But the time had not yet arrived, and I didn't know when it would. For some weird reason, it felt good to face that reality. I took a deep breath and told the truth.

"I know I've made a lot of mistakes," I prayed out loud, while my neighbor watering her flowers gave me a triple take. "I've felt entitled to things before I've earned them. From my career aspirations to my home to my clothes to my trips—I've always demanded to live outside our means, buying things we couldn't afford to impress people I don't even like." I huffed and puffed up a hill. "I know Rob has gone along with much of it to make me happy, but now we're in massive debt, exhausted, depressed, and scared," I said as my lip trembled. "I'm not a victim; I'm a spoiled brat, who always wants more and more and more when I've already been given so much." I waved hello at another concerned neighbor. "I am so, so sorry," I said, tears dripping off my chin. "From now on, I take responsibility. I'll treasure and steward what I've been given and earned, instead of feeling entitled to more. I believe you'll provide a roof over our heads, a roof we can afford—and it will be wonderful. Thank you, thank you, thank you." And I continued to say thank you all the way home, as tears slipped down my neck, drenching my collar.

It would be one of the last times I'd walk into our home. Dodging half-filled boxes, I slipped up to our room so Rob wouldn't see me and worry. I felt incredible relief owning it and accepting the consequences. Instead of resisting, I chose to simply believe it would be all right. Bruce Lee taught that we should be "formless, shapeless, like water."[3] That's what surrender felt like to me. I could just flow like water and trust where I was going was good.

And besides, I still had my arms and legs. We'd be fine.

My phone pinged with an email. It was a notification a new house was on the market. I received many throughout the day, so I didn't think much of it. The picture pulled up, and my hair blew back like I'd bit into a York Peppermint Pattie. I gazed at a delightfully remodeled '60s home, modern and vintage and everything I ever wanted. A renowned architect had turned it into the coolest house I had ever seen. Her homes were coveted and hard to get, and there was one, in my inbox, right on time. The price had dropped dramatically, but it was still out of our range. I texted my agent, Crystal, anyway because you never know. Within a half hour, she called me back. "Okay, here's the deal," she said. "I just called the agent. This house has been remodeled so over the top that it won't appraise, so she's only been accepting cash offers." I groaned. "Wait. Hold on," she continued. "She's accepted two separate cash offers, but both have fallen through in the final stages—that's why it just popped back up on the market with such a huge price drop." I steadied myself on my dresser. "She's done messing around. She said if you want to come see it and make an offer, they'll cancel tomorrow's open house."

"But it's still out of our price range," I said.

"I know. I told the agent she has to meet us in the middle, and they've agreed to negotiate. If you want it, you can have it," she said with a squeal.

"Crystal," I said soberly, "I'm not sure if we're at the place in our professional relationship where we're ready to say I love you. But I just wanted to say . . . I love you."

"I love you too. Now let's go look at your new house."

I knew I had another iPhone charger somewhere. I could see it in my mind's eye. It was in a ziplock bag, along with dried-out pens and birthday cards I didn't really want but didn't have the heart to throw away. We had been in our new house for quite some time, but whenever I've moved into a new place, there's always been a handful of boxes that never get unpacked. Instead they get stacked in some kind of storage room, waiting for sweaty men to someday move them to another home.

After an aggressive search, I concluded those boxes were the only place the spare charger could be. I opened up the first one, and there on top was a wooden box. I opened it, and inside were all of my old fears. After a quick scan for spiders, I sat down next to the box and read each fear, one by one.

My first fear was the one that had led right to where I was sitting—fear that after being told I had less than a month to pack up and leave, we wouldn't find anything good to move into. Little did I know a renowned architect had already built us the most delightful home, and it was just waiting for us to move in. But what I really didn't see coming was the flood. Within six months after our move, Nebraska would experience historic rain and ice melt. As the rivers rose, so did the lake. Up, up, up to the beach of the home I had so desperately wanted to be my own, bashing up against the doors, rushing into the lower level, rising to the ceiling. Then up, up, up the stairs, whooshing its way to the main floor, as dead fish and debris and catastrophe claimed ownership of the house my family had once occupied. The same house that didn't qualify for flood insurance.

And that was just my first fear—there were more. I was afraid my treasured dream of becoming a book author would never come true. I feared if it did come true, the book would bomb. I feared I'd lose my agent. I feared having no friends. I feared if I failed much longer, I wouldn't have the strength to keep trying. I feared if I lost my strength, my family would be in poverty, always insecure, with no rest or safety. I feared I didn't know who I was. I feared I was a fraud. I feared mediocrity. Lost opportunities. That deep down, I didn't want the dream, just the applause. I feared I was selfish, stupid, and mean. I feared our debt would never get paid. I feared I'd fall out of love with Rob, or worse, he'd fall out of love with me. I feared dying too soon. I feared dying alone. I feared something bad happening to my babies. I feared I'd always be fat. I feared I'd never stop caring about being fat. I feared Rob would die. I feared my parents would die too. I feared I'd be alone like an orphan, with no one to love me so unconditionally again. I feared that one day I'd get a huge wart near my eye that would not only look hideous but obstruct my vision. I feared people would hate me. I feared bad reviews. I feared wrinkles and crepey knees. I feared karma didn't know the address of my enemies. I feared all my hard work would be for nothing. The list went on, but I didn't need to read more.

All those fears, I thought, while ripping the cards in half. *And not a single one came true.*

I got up, dusted off my butt, and leaned against the dryer. True, I still had a lot of life to live; the shoe could still drop, and eventually, some would. But after reading my list again, I decided I wouldn't fear the end of the world until the world actually ends.

And even then, I thought as I turned to leave, *I bet God sends a train to come get me.*

FOURTEEN

DANCE CARDIO

———

Uhhhh. What are you doing?" Lucy asked, her hair wild, mermaid nightgown tucked into the back of her underwear. Poppy was on Lucy's right side, her thick strawberry hair matted on the back of her head, as if she had teased that spot and sprayed it firm with Aussie Mega Hold.

"What's it look like I'm doing?" I shot back. The truth is, I had no idea what I was doing, but I wasn't about to give her the satisfaction. Rob was supposed to be playing interference, by the way, and was nowhere to be found. "If the girls wake up before I'm done working out, don't let them interrupt me, I have to concentrate," I said. "I won't," he said. Yet, there they were.

"Where's your father?" I panted.

"I dunno," Lucy said.

"Daddy not upstairs," Poppy chimed in. I could tell they felt the spectacle before them was very disconcerting, like the smell of marijuana on a nun's habit. I was bouncing around aimlessly, puffy, red, and breathless. I'm not a sweater, I just sort of sweat internally until I swell up as if I'm having an allergic reaction to latex. My feet touched the ground on every beat, my boobs smacked against my lower abdomen every third. I was kicking, pumping, high-stepping, sideswiping, karate chopping, and sashaying.

"Who's that lady?" Lucy asked.

"Tracy Anderson," I puffed.

"What's she doing?"

"Dance cardio."

"Aren't you supposed to be doing what she's doing?"

Lucy had seen this before. A few months prior she'd caught me doing a yoga lesson off Amazon Prime Video. My back was tight, so I perused yoga videos and found a few beginner ones. Lucy learned within just a few moments you're supposed to do what the person on the screen is doing and that, by the looks of it, her mother was doing whatever she wanted.

"Yes, baby," I huffed. "You girls go upstairs and find Daddy," Then I grapevined across the room, topping it off with a kick-in-the-jewels leg thrust before grapevining my way the other direction.

I know it's a parenting cliché, but I miss being able to live my life in private without someone taking it as an affront. Or crying so hard about it that I'm the one who has to console them. If a woman is ever asked, "Why you putting that cotton thingy up your butt?" you know that poor woman's personal space has been violated. And that's exactly what I had to deal with when both my children insisted on being present while I peed on one otherwise benign Saturday afternoon.

"It's a tampon, and it didn't go up my butt. It went into my girl privates, called a vagina," I said while Lucy innocently and lovingly caressed the top of my bare thighs. "Our butt is in the back. We've been over this, Lu Lu."

"But you didn't put it in your privates; you put it up your butt."

"I didn't put it up my butt."

"Yes, you did. I saw you do it. You put it up your butt."

"I put it up my vagina, not my butt."

"Why?"

"Every month, if there's no baby in my tummy," I began, as if narrating a documentary, "the blood that is there to help make the baby is released. I use a tampon to catch the blood."

"Blood comes out of your butt?"

"IT'S NOT MY BUTT!"

"Goo goo butt," Poppy said, laughing, trying to use the pants around my ankles as a stepping stool to climb into my lap.

Everyone warned me when I got pregnant that I would never again poop in peace. I believed them, but more in a "haha how funny" sort of way. I didn't actually think that it would be years before I could go to the bathroom without an audience. And they don't just observe from a close distance; they task me, make snack requests, and put their tablet in my face because the PBS KIDS app isn't working. They try to sit on my lap, make clinical observations about my pores ("Why you got big holes on your face?"), then make their way to the shower and grab a razor while I dole out idle threats. It's humiliating is what it is.

I don't want my life narrated. This isn't *The Wonder Years*. And I find when a child narrates and inquires about your every move, it puts you on the defense because cascading, nonjudgmental-yet-moderately-offensive observations are getting thrown at you like darts. "Why you got a fuzzy butt?" Poppy asked once. "It's not my butt; you know that. And it's fuzzy because it gets fuzzy as you get older and become a grown-up like Mommy. Now, let me enjoy my shower. AND ROB! I THOUGHT YOU WERE WRANGLING THEM!" I may not be the best teacher, but I swear I've clearly taught them age-appropriate anatomy. Yet, somehow, it's all a butt with these two.

"Well, in their defense," Rob once said, "it does sort of look like a butt." He's right, I suppose.

Our renovated 1960s house has its original doors. They close and lock, but it takes a little finesse and upward lift to make sure the latch is set in. One day I got the decadent idea to take a bath and failed to properly finesse and lift. We have only one bath in the house, used mostly by the girls. After cleaning out an entire chest worth of toys and scrubbing off a worrisome film, I slipped into a hot bath brimming with mint-infused Epsom salts. As I settled in and rested my head on a rolled-up towel, my girls busted in like a SWAT team. The door gave way easier than expected, so they tumbled in. Once they composed themselves, they froze, and I noticed a subtle yet rapid eye movement as if their brains were inputting data. There was their mother, naked in their bathtub, and I saw synapses connecting and lifelong, dreadful memories forming.

"What you doing, Mama?" Lucy asked.

"I'm taking a bath, sweetheart. Now, you girls leave me be. I'll be out in a little while."

"Mama, you got *big* boob boobs!" Poppy said.

"Big, *big* boob boobs!" Lucy added. A few years back, I watched some reality show documentary, in the vein of *My 600-lb Life*, and there was a thin woman whose boobs, in a bra, hung below the top of her thighs. Her cup was a double Z. I had no idea bras went up the entire alphabet, so I leaned in, intrigued. She was getting a reduction, to a measly, teeny, triple K. And her husband, with long, sweaty blond hair underneath a baseball cap, held her hand and wept. Not because he was concerned about her going into surgery but because he was mourning her boobs. "That's what attracted me to her," he stammered out between sobs. Thankfully, the surgery was a success, and boobs that were once at her thighs were now at her belly button. Her husband, however, was still in mourning.

My point is—my boobs aren't *that* big. I can still shop in a physical store without going online, although I have to admit that my selection is often thin. Still, I recognized the same expression on my children's faces that I'd had watching that episode—shock, awe, and a slight tingle of disgust. Finally, Rob appeared in the doorway, breathless, like a person who thinks they've lost their children. "Girls, there you are! Let Mommy be. Let's give her privacy," he said, ushering them as if directing traffic. "Come on, get out. Let's go."

Poppy burst into tears and tried to climb into the bathtub with me as if she were being taken away to an orphanage. As Rob swooped her up and took her away, arms stretched, screaming,

I lay back on my towel, determined to relax. My mind wandered to the time, many years ago, when my niece Zoey was spending the night at my mom's house. Zoey was the Queen of Offensive Observations. You never knew what would come out of that child's mouth, so you often took great care to look your best around her. My mom discreetly washed off her makeup while Zoey was distracted in the tub, but she was caught while drying her face. "Nani," Zoey said, curious, surrounded by bubbles, "you remind me of someone." Dread formed at the tip of my mom's head and poured to her toes. "I know who it is!" Zoey shouted, slapping the water with her hand. "You remind me of an old lady!"

They don't mean to hurt us. What in the world is self-loathing? Self-doubt? How could one possibly be insecure? Aren't we all just so delightful, just as we are? Big boobs, fuzzy butts, old-lady faces and all?

They're right, of course. We are. But soon enough, they'll change their minds.

We all do.

There's always been this part of me that can't just enjoy an activity; I have to be the best at the activity. Particularly athletic activities. This kind of perseverance and determination would normally be admirable. The only trouble is, I typically quit ten days in due to quads so sore I need handrails to get off the toilet.

In my twenties while working in Northern California, I was about thirty pounds overweight. Instead of combating this by starting out with the obvious, like cutting out daily happy hour cocktails and fried appetizers, I instead enrolled in some kind of gimmicky boot camp, hosted by an ex-marine. I can only speak for myself, but all the drama, screaming, crying, falling off treadmills, and throwing up in trash cans that we enjoyed watching on *The Biggest Loser* could be found in this boot camp. There was no easing in and getting the body acclimated; there was just going all in, crying, throwing up, and dragging your leg behind you as made your way back to your car.

After the first boot camp, my quads and glutes were so sore the next morning that at least three people asked if I had sprained my ankle. After a meeting, I went into a unisex restroom that was not handicap accessible and couldn't get off the toilet. My arms were fatigued and limp but, thankfully, still had a little fight in them. The problem was, there was nothing I could grab onto to give me some lift. The sink was out of reach, and the toilet paper holder was low. I'm not exaggerating when I tell you that I couldn't get off the toilet. If a T. rex had stomped into the building and ripped off the roof, adrenaline would have done its darndest to pry my butt off the toilet, but it would have failed. My quads were worthless, and the hot sweats of panic were fast approaching.

My only option was to roll off the toilet, onto a urine-covered floor, crawl to the sink, then use my arms to lift myself up to a standing position. Once that mission was accomplished, I locked my knees in place, then exited the bathroom, stiff, like a toy soldier. "Did you sprain your ankle?" the secretary asked as I was leaving.

This tends to be my pattern when it comes to physical fitness. I demand 150 percent focus, grit, and determination from myself, then slowly limp away when I realize life's too short for lactic acid. Considering this, why I attempted Tracy Anderson's method is still a mystery to me. But I immediately jumped into the deep end and committed to giving her a full thirty days before I'd even flirt with quitting. I was drawn to her method because it's supposed to create a more feminine, ballerina-type body rather than, say, a bulky, more masculine body. Without exercise, I would say I have an "only woman on the roadwork crew" body, so I try not to glorify it with my workouts whenever possible.

Tracy's method requires mat work that demands muscle exhaustion in weird positions. When you're done screaming through your 1,035th cockeye leg lift, you are supposed to do her dance cardio for thirty minutes. Except, Tracy is a bit odd in that she doesn't give you cues or repeat a move enough times to let you get the hang of what she's doing. You end up looking like Lucille Ball after sneaking onstage at Copacabana. You're dressed for the part, but you're mostly looking around, way off cue, bumping into things, hopping and flailing, with a heart rate up so high you fear cardiac arrest. This is just Tracy's "thing," and you're supposed to accept it until you get used to it.

While I wanted to humiliate myself in private, Rob encouraged me to let the girls be with me. He thought it was good for them to see us exercise and watch us eat healthfully. He was about three weeks into a keto diet, with moderate success, which is usually the time he waxes poetic about the state of obesity in America and how we should do everything we can to set a good, healthy example for our girls and for all American citizens in general.

I'm no different, really. Typically, if I've been on a diet for a few weeks and have lost enough weight for my pants to feel moderately loose, I'll get cocky, as if I've arrived, and start to coach disinterested friends and family on health and fitness. "Weight loss is 80 percent diet," I'll say, sipping freshly squeezed kale juice, "but I don't care about weight loss. I care about my health and living well for a long time, for my children and their children and, God willing, their children." Then some will nod in appreciation before asking the one thing they actually care about: "But how much weight did you lose the first week?"

My relationship with my body is complex and often contradictory. There's the practical side of me that simply acknowledges that being overweight doesn't feel good. I don't like how it feels when my cleavage and neck are an inch apart. I don't like the feeling of tight pants or that my daughters often use my muffin top as a stepping stool or chair. I also don't like taking fifty-seven selfies until finally landing on one decent enough to put on Instagram. Who has that kind of time?

Then, of course, there's the vengeful side of me that simply wants to be thin so I can really stick it to my enemies. My playful side wants to drink beer and eat pizza carefree, like everyone else. My apathetic side doesn't really care that much and is perfectly fine wearing loose pajama bottoms to Target. And my ambitious side wants to be in the best shape of my life, just to say I did it. Just so I can win.

And I can be all of these sides throughout one day, or even, most often, all at once.

Rob and I were both chubby kids well through middle school, and with that gigantic bummer, we try hard to hit the right balance. We don't want our own insecurities from childhood to spill over onto our girls. We want them to have confidence in who they are, no matter their size. But we also want to guide them toward a healthy, active life. We want them to feel good, strong, and healthy. We know the dangers of childhood obesity and want to shield them from the crisis. But I guess I've found that some wounds run so deep, if you unwrap years upon years of gauze, you'll uncover a festered, oozy wound that just can't get over the pain of being a fat kid. And you just want your babies to be spared.

Oh, how I wish I could evolve! Or perhaps we could all devolve and go back to the Victorian era, when big and fluffy was hot and sexy. Your girth implied wealth, health, and prosperity, unlike those gangly peasants who could feel their hip bones. How I would have thrived! But, alas, here I am in modern times, where we throw parades celebrating everyone's beauty, regardless of size, then go home and avoid looking at ourselves in the mirror. Lena Dunham says she isn't body positive, more like body tolerant. I know how she feels.

I wish I could teleport a woman who had real problems into twenty-first-century America. Like a woman from the medieval times. Or pluck a woman off the Oregon Trail and have her stay in my house for the weekend. I'd give her a tour and stop by the toilet. "No dying from feces-related deaths up in here, sister!" Then I'd open the medicine cabinet, sigh, and say breathlessly, "Oh, we don't die from silly things anymore. We have antibiotics." Then she'd look in my refrigerator, packed so full we had to get a freezer for our basement, and notice all the condiments. Even multiples of the same thing. "I can never remember if I have mustard, so I just get another one," I'd say with a chuckle.

Then she'd turn on the kitchen sink and look at me with

eyes wide enough to fall out. "Is this water clean? No cholera?" she'd ask.

"Sure is," I'd say. "Super clean and safe. Except not safe enough, so I buy spring water from the store."

Shocked, she'd wonder out loud, "Does anyone die of starvation?"

And I'd scoff, "Oh dear, no. In fact, our number-one killer is that we eat too much!" Then I'd laugh and laugh while she stood there blinking.

Not quite done with her ridiculous questions, she'd ask, "Where's your husband? Is he out tilling the field?"

And I'd giggle, of course. "Oh, Laura—he doesn't even mow the lawn."

Eventually she'd make her way to the family room and pause at a table with my family photos. It would remind her of her own babies she lost to various common diseases we don't deal with anymore, like mumps or typhoid fever. She'd reflect on how it was a miracle if any of her children made it past five years old, and here mine lived to that age with such ease. Then she'd look over at me to observe the new, modern woman. I'd look back at her and, with sadness in my eyes, ask, "Do you think my thighs look too cottage cheesy in these shorts?"

Then she'd beg to be teleported home.

"But you not doing what she doing," Lucy said with her hands on her hips.

"Well, what she's doing is insane!" I huffed and puffed, kicked and jumped. Tracy Anderson had lost her mind.

Gradually, Lucy inched her way closer to my flailing limbs. "Can I dance with you?"

Begging for a bit of relief, I conceded. "Sure, baby, come on," I said. We moved together, bumped into each other, and she said, "Mommy, look!" at least thirty times while doing various indistinguishable arm movements.

"I dance too!" Poppy said, jumping from the couch.

"Come on, Pop, let's dance!" I shouted.

We hopped around, twirled, leaped, high kicked, and moon-walked. I threw in a few pelvic thrusts, as that's my signature move. Tracy continued on, encouraging us to keep trying, keep dancing—and so we did. But in our own way, burning far fewer calories.

We were three of the happiest, most beautiful, most terrible dancers you had ever seen. And in that precious, rare moment, there were no wounds to unwrap, no detrimental thoughts to unpack. We were just ourselves, us three. In love. Gorgeous, perfect, and free.

FIFTEEN

ALMOST MURDERED

I n the light of the moon, I saw Rob leap out of bed. His arm was cocked back like a pistol ready to shoot. Survival mode is a fascinating state of mind. I suppose I can only speak for myself, but instead of leaping into immediate action, my brain does a quick scan—robotic, even—downloading information, searching for clues. Within seconds I've determined whether the situation is worthy of a scream or if I can just shrug and move on.

My heart was lodged so deep in my throat as I scanned our room that I was wheezy. Was there a murderer in my midst? And, similarly, WAS THIS THE END?

Once my eyes adjusted and thoroughly surveyed the situation, the only person I saw in the room was Rob—winding up to punch our wall clock.

I'd like to believe that, in general, I am a kind and compassionate person. However, when the rubber meets the road, it honestly just depends. As it applies to sleepwalkers and sleep talkers, I will have none of it. I know it's not the sleeper's fault, but that's irrelevant. I will not be soothing, gently lulling the sleeper back to bed. I want to be that person, the kind that sees the sleeper as a helpless victim, taking care to get them back to bed, safe and sound. But no. If you wake me and freak me out with your nonsense, I will launch into a waterfall of obscenities. I will defend myself from your lunacy, and I will shame you into taking your creepy butt back to bed. I don't even know where all of this aggression is coming from—all I know is that survival is my number-one priority.

In college Jen talked in her sleep every time we had a sleepover. We were both resident advisors, and one night while we were on duty, we fell asleep on her futon, watching *Clueless*. Eventually the movie ended, and in the stillness of her room, I jolted awake as if from a nightmare. My eyes shot open, and I looked directly into hers. She was glaring at me, her head hovered over mine, her long hair tickling the side of my face. She was propped up on her elbow and started tenderly stroking my cheek. "You having a good time, sweetheart?" she said with a sickly sweet voice. "You having a good time?" What made Jen the absolute worst is that she spoke coherently, as if possessed, and never wavered off script as some sleepers do because, well, they're asleep.

"What are you talking about?" I said, gripping her wrist.

"What do you mean, silly?" she said sweetly and eerily, like some kind of nanny raised from the dead. "I'm asking if you're having a good time."

"You're a freak. Unhand me!" I ripped her gentle fingers from my face.

"Geeeeeeeez," she said, rolling her eyes. "Have it your way!" Then she rolled over and slipped into a peaceful, gentle sleep. Meanwhile, I was flat on my back, panting like someone hiding from a sniper. I slipped out of her room in the cover of darkness, to the safety and refuge of my own bed. The next morning, I called her up. "So," I said, popping a pretzel into my mouth. "You sleep good last night?"

"Yeah, really good," she said. "Why'd you leave?"

"I'm the one asking the questions," I said, crunching louder than I meant to into the mouthpiece. "Do you remember what you were dreaming about last night?"

"Ummmm." She took a moment to ponder. "I think I was dreaming about my baby sister coming up to visit. Why?"

"I'll tell you why," I said, pausing for effect. "You woke me up, stroking my face, staring at me with dead, evil eyes. You're terrifying!"

These sorts of things happened to me and Jen so often during the course of our best friendship, I started to get anxiety every time she fell asleep. Years later, after we were both married and had children, we took a quick trip together to New York. I woke up to her staring at me by the side of my bed. "Have you packed yet?" she said coldly. "We gotta go."

"You gotta go to hell," I told her. "Now get back to bed and shut up."

"Geeeeeeez," she said, rolling her eyes. "Have it your way!"

But thankfully, Rob woke up midswing, mostly because I was

cussing like a Navy SEAL instructor so loudly that he didn't have a choice. He realized he was about to destroy my clearanced Isaac Mizrahi clock, apologized, and slipped back into bed. "Sorry," he said again, laying his head on his pillow. "I think I dreamed someone was in our room." Did his apology cause my heart to wiggle out of my throat back into its proper place? No, but we could discuss that in the morning.

Just as I began to drift back to sleep, a loud, booming crash sounded inside our home. If I could describe the sound, it was as if a desk had been flipped over.

I screamed out in total, unbridled terror.

Someone is murdering me for real this time! Rob wasn't dreaming; he was responding to something real. Something that's now in my house, about to make me the star of a hit Netflix murder documentary.

I like to believe that I have a feminine, damsel-in-distress scream like actresses do in the movies. But the high-pitched kind actually takes a lot of energy to belt out, and when facing your mortality, who has the time? No, no. My screams are low, gritty, and throaty—like a blend of Joan Rivers and James Earl Jones trying to shout down a guy who's running off with a purse.

That is the sound I delivered into the night.

Rob and I flew out of bed so forcefully that I think our comforter got whipped up in the ceiling fan. We ran into the family room, and from there, Rob ran into the kitchen to grab a knife.

Truth be told, we don't have great knives in the house. Years ago I sprung for some Cutco knives, but they're so dull now that I haven't been able to cut a tomato in years. You're supposedly able to send them back in for a good sharpen for free, but who in their right mind would do such a thing? I have no less than ten ill-fitting articles of clothing with the tags on hanging up in my closet—because actually leaving my home, with a box, driving, parking, and waiting in line to ship these items back is somewhere near "scrub the base of the toilet" on my to-do list.

Other than the Cutco knives, we have cheap steak knives Rob brought into the marriage from his bachelor days. He probably picked them up at Walmart, and over a decade into our marriage, they're just about one notch above a butter knife. Rob slid into the kitchen and picked up the first one he saw—the one I used right before bed to slice off a hunk of ham for a little snack. It was on the cutting board and still had pieces of ham and mustard on it. If the knife could even break skin, which was doubtful, I was at least assured the mustard would sting the murderer real bad.

Rob went on his search throughout the house. As a woman, I've thought through every survival scenario. After I had the girls, my strategizing went into overdrive. Years upon years of watching violent, murdery, kidnappy movies and documentaries hasn't helped and has admittedly set my imagination ablaze. I take my survival plans seriously. I have a plan A, B, C, and D in my arsenal should an emergency be taking place. But already, I was two minutes into an attempted murder, and my whole alphabet plan had gone to crap.

During previous house discussions, I explicitly forbade Rob from searching the house alone because if he did run into a murderer and they killed him, I'd be next in line to save us, and I don't even scream right, let alone kill right. If he was hiding safely behind some wall with us, then worst-case scenario, we could use his body as a shield. Look, that may seem like I'm being heartless, but I'm simply talking about biological, raw, maternal survival. Now's not the time to make it personal.

The trouble was, I didn't have sufficient evidence to raise the alarm to almost-murdered levels. Calling 911, waking up the girls, hiding in a closet, and waiting for police sirens to tear through our sleepy neighborhood was a lot of work, so I felt I needed a bit more to go on than a *boom*. That's why I made the split-second decision to allow Rob to search our darkened, quiet house with a knife covered in ham and mustard, alone. I just prayed those weren't my famous last words.

Afraid to wake the girls over nothing, yet still wanting to protect them somehow, I stood in front of their bedroom door, trying to figure out what to do with my hands. Having my arms hang listless by my side didn't seem to rise to the occasion, so I tried propping one hand on my hip. That didn't really seem to fit the bill either, but it did arouse some confidence, so I went with it.

I heard footsteps coming toward me and let out a long, slow sigh when Rob emerged from the basement.

"Anything?"

"No, nothing."

"Did you see furniture tipped over?"

"Nope."

"Did we dream it?"

"Uh, like—both of us?" Rob said, shifting to a less aggressive grip on the knife. "No."

We reluctantly headed back to our bedroom when, suddenly,

Rob put his arm out to stop me. I held my breath tight as my mind shuffled through various ways I could push Rob in front of the murderer, grab the girls, and run for our lives. Again, nothing personal.

With the hammy knife, he pointed to the bathroom. There it was. A large bag of toys we stick on the shower wall above the girls' bathtub had fallen and crashed into the tub.

That's why I screamed into the night. That's why Rob scoured the house with a dull mustard-covered knife in his underwear. That's why I sacrificed my husband at the hands of a murderer in my mind.

In our defense, the bag was big, and the boom was *freakishly* loud, okay?

"The suction cup on that thing leaves a lot to be desired," I muttered.

Rob nodded. We stood, quietly. A little bit embarrassed but mostly pissed we'd lost good sleep.

"Want some ham?" Rob asked. We went into the kitchen and pulled out a leftover ham bone. This particular ham was worth the trouble. Maybe it was the glaze; who knows.

I checked on the girls, who were both lying still like vampires, yet breathing softly, completely unmoved by the chaos that had swirled around them.

Bruno, our English bulldog, just lay there like a sausage, blinking drowsily, judging us.

We may not have been almost murdered, but I was warmed by a simple truth—Rob would risk his life to protect his girls, without hesitation. And I'd let him.

SIXTEEN

SHEETS FOR CURTAINS

The first sad moment in my life that I recall is the stain. My dad and brother had been carrying boxes when my mom opened the door. We were greeted by a sea of black, greasy, shiny oil on the carpet. We had rented this house from someone who had kept his motorcycle in the living room—if that gives you any kind of visual as to what we were dealing with. That was the first time I saw my mom cry.

I, on the other hand, had been buzzing all morning. In the new place, I would share a room with my older sister, a major win and a leg up from the large room I'd occupied in our last house, where monsters lurked in my closet. I was too little to fully grasp the gravity of the moment on my own. I sensed it was new and different, but it all felt okay. I think.

But when my mom covered her face and cried into the palm of her hands, it was the first time I wondered if maybe it wasn't okay at all. I looked at my family for cues. I searched their eyes, their expressions, the way they talked and their tone. *Maybe it's worse than I think.*

Mom rushed into the kitchen, filled a bucket with hot water and soap, and brought it back to the living room. She got on her hands and knees and scrubbed the oil stain as my dad and brother maneuvered around her, carrying the couch. I started to doubt whether this was as exciting as I had hoped. *The oil stain is bad—but guys, I get to share a room with my big sister. I hope we can see this is the best thing to ever happen to me.*

I helped my family move in by sitting on the furniture they were trying to set up while playing my Game Boy. Everyone seemed okay, more or less. I'm sure there was grief behind closed doors I wasn't privy to. No one lied to me; the truth was known. But it was still our family, together. Our circumstances were different, but we were still the same.

As we moved all our things in, my parents ordered pizza (*could this day get any better!*), and afterward I observed my dad while he watched an old episode of *Matlock*. Was he worried? Did he seem scared? Was this really bad?

But he seemed to be daydreaming, tapping his foot and humming a tune.

I could breathe.

Sometimes horrible things happen. Life doesn't stop, so we're forced to wake up and get on with it. So many times there isn't anything we've done to cause our misfortune or anything we can do to stop it. People take our investments and disappear. Tornadoes turn a house to rubble. A spouse packs a bag and leaves. A flood washes it all away. And life as you know it, just like that, is gone.

Yet we keep waking up each morning. The sun keeps rising. It's terribly annoying, but I guess it helps to keep our recovery on schedule.

My mom was on her tippy-toes, covering our windows with white sheets because we didn't have curtains. She pinned one side up with a tack, the second tack between her teeth. Her mood seemed lighter, loving. We were all going to be okay.

I remember very little else during this time, but I remember their moods vividly. That tells me their moods mattered to me most. Not the style of roof that covered our heads or that my mom had to sell some of my more expensive toys. Not our furniture, curtains, or a stain on the carpet. I cared about how they were feeling. And if they were okay, it gave me confidence to be okay too.

Hope, I guess, is all I remember.

Within only about five years, my dad would become one of the most celebrated home builders in Omaha, known and sought after for his incredible craftsmanship. I had become a teenager by then, and during a fight with my mom, I yelled and screamed, then stomped up to my room and slammed the door. That's when Dad got involved. Not because I had disrespected my mother, but because I had slammed the door and hurt the wood. It's just who he is. His deep respect and natural talent for turning a piece of wood into a work of art has always been with him. How can a blueprint transform into a beautiful home? I've never understood it. I've learned from him that details matter. Doing the work, to completion, to the best of your ability—matters. Never leave work undone. Respect even the smallest detail and make it beautiful.

After that move to the rental house, my mom never scrubbed motor oil off a carpet again. She's lived like a queen ever since.

I've experienced loss many different times in many different ways in my life. I draw from those moments when I'm afraid it could happen again. My dad's light hum, my mom's tippy-toes, and the loving way she glanced at me while I watched her. Everyone will experience some sort of disaster in their lives, and my parents experienced theirs with dignity. So even if I don't feel like it, even if my chin trembles—I hold it high. I pay attention to detail. I get the job done and respect the work of my hands.

Recently I asked my mom what it was really like for them during that time. When life as they knew it ended and they had to start anew. She said she would lie with me in my twin-sized bed, hum me to sleep, and feel comforted even within the fear and uncertainty. While there was much to grieve, and she grieved privately a lot, there was a sense they would overcome it. That it was a moment in time. A hard, terrible, but temporary moment. And they were right. It was.

Almost every day during the self-quarantine of a global pandemic, I've thought about that time in the teeny town house. The oil stain, the sheets for curtains.

This morning, over coffee, I chatted with my mom and said,

a little sarcastically, "I wonder what my girls will remember about a pandemic."

"You," she said, pausing to take a sip. "They'll mostly remember you."

SEVENTEEN

THE GINGERBREAD MAN

W hy does it say the little old lady is little if she's old?" Lucy asked. She kept trying to reposition herself by digging her elbow into my right boob. Poppy was sitting not on my lap, but one step above, comfortably on my muffin top.

"She's old, but she's little in size," I said, pushing her elbow off my boob. "May I continue?" Lucy nodded and settled in. Every night I read them a story in their bedroom. They used to have their own rooms, until about a month prior, when I was complaining on the phone with my mom about how miserable it was writing in my basement office. It's a finished basement, designed and decorated nicely, but it's so cold down there it makes your heart stop the minute you take your foot off the final step. Summer is worse than winter because the air conditioner acts like a whipping snowstorm, licking its way off ice caps right into your face. What's weird is that we have all the vents closed, so no one can figure out where the chill is coming from. It's probably because we're too busy doing that hyperventilating thing people do when they submerge themselves too quickly in a swimming pool.

But even so, I could make do with a huge fur robe and slippers on occasion. But what really turned me off was when Rob started working from home and needed a quiet room to hold Zoom meetings in without the higher-ups hearing "Daddy toot and make a poopy in his undies!" in the background, followed by uproarious laughter, and then eventually someone crying because they tripped and fell into a doorjamb.

Once Rob moved into my office, it was tainted, and I never felt the same way in it again. Writers—actually, just women in general—need a space of their own. A nook, a corner, or if the husband is passive, the entire house will do just fine. But somewhere there needs to be a door that locks, a place of refuge, where a woman can embrace twenty full minutes where everyone gets their freakin' hands off her.

Once my writing actually became a thing people were reading, I rewarded myself with an extremely large desk from Pottery Barn, fashioned to look like a carpenter's workbench. It was somehow neither masculine nor feminine and made me feel all cozy like it was connecting me to my home-building father. It became a sacred place for me to hone my love of writing, and it's the kind of desk that looks expensive because it is. Throughout our entire marriage, in fact, it was the first piece of furniture we purchased that hadn't come in a box and been assembled by me and Rob, hunched over a sea of screws, both of us cussing because we screwed an entire section on backward and had to take it apart again.

But that was the kind of cheap, wobbly desk he moved into my chilly creative space. It was tucked in the corner, and he piled things on top of it, like random papers, computer wires, empty LaCroix cans, and the box his laptop came in. I'd sit there at my masterful desk, wrap my robe made of grizzly bear hide around my body, gaze at his crappy work corner, and immediately have inspiration and creativity sucked right out of me. One time, I guess because he needed more room, I caught him sitting at my desk, in my delicate chair that his large six-foot-three body barely fit in, and was gravely offended. My sacred place, defiled! It's the same reason I've been warned not to touch baby birds—once the mother catches your scent, she just flies off to make a new family. But we couldn't afford another desk, so I had to eventually get over it.

It was harder than it should have been. Once I've lost respect for something, there's really no finding it. Soon, my own desk became a catchall for random crap I didn't know what to do with but didn't want to get rid of, like a large vase that was too big for normal flowers or the girls' artwork I didn't want displayed but didn't want to throw away either. Lucy's first tooth sat there for weeks in that ziplock bag while I tried to figure out if it should go in a scrapbook, a memory box, or maybe just in the trash can. I still haven't decided.

So, once my beloved desk became a place where unwanted

objects could rest elevated off the ground, I began writing upstairs on the couch. But my accessibility on the couch attracted children, who were usually hungry or bored or just wanted to drape all over me like a wet blanket. I needed a plan B.

"Why don't you put the girls together in Poppy's room?" my mom said. "They'll love it, and you can make Lucy's room your office." Though the thought intrigued and excited me, I wasn't so sure. Lucy loves her privacy, often closing her door and playing quietly on her own. But to be fair, she really wasn't contributing financially to the household, and her room would make the perfect office. In fact, when we bought the house, it was staged as one. The room gets good light and is very inviting, with built-in shelves and just enough space for my large desk. It was also upstairs, where the temperature could sustain life, and near the kitchen, where I could refill my coffee. That was it; my mind was made up. Within the hour, I was dragging mattresses through the hallway.

One of the perks of having the girls in one room is that we can have our nighttime ritual together at the same time. It's the most precious part of my day, but I'm also exhausted, so I'm not trying to make it last. We put on a dim lamp, pull the blankets down, and climb in together, very cozy. The child whose bed we're not in will remind me at least thirteen times that we'll be reading in her bed tomorrow; then they claw and catfight over who gets to sit in my lap. The loser has to sit next to me, which is actually far more comfortable but a less dominant and victorious position, which is why it isn't favored. Then, of course, they fight over what book we're going to read. Each is allowed to choose one, where I veto at least three, especially the Disney movie-adaptation books that are edited so far down you can barely grasp the plot, yet are so long Rob asks where I've been when I finally emerge from their bedroom after reading one.

After we've decided on the book, one or all three of us get up to pee; then inevitably someone asks for a snack. A banana, preferably, as long as it isn't too brown. And if it is too brown, toast with butter will do. After I tell them they've lost their minds, we settle in for a good read.

We've been on a *Gingerbread Man* kick lately. It feels like a book that should only be read during the winter season, so I'm a little bothered reading it in the muggy heat of summer. I shouldn't complain, though, because they finally stopped requesting *Olaf's Night Before Christmas* sometime in June. Reading it before bed with the sun still out, cicadas humming, and neighbor kids outside bouncing basketballs felt almost morally corrupt—like Starbucks trying to roll out Pumpkin Spice Lattes in April. But they would beg, and I would be desperate to get the day over with, so alas, Santa visited Elsa's castle, and we chased the Gingerbread Man.

"Run! Run! As fast as you can!" I said passionately. "You can't catch me! I'm the Gingerbread Man!"

"Why can't they catch him?" Poppy asked.

"Because he's fast."

"He's a cookie. How fast can he be?" Lucy pondered.

"Fast enough. Okay, here we go . . . 'The little old man reached down to grab him, but quick as a wink, the Gingerbread Man ran out the door—'"

"What that say?" Poppy pointed her chubby finger at the bottom right corner of the page.

"It's the number twelve. 'And down the road, and the little old man and the little old woman ran after him—'"

"Why it say twelve?"

"It's the page number, baby. Can we continue, please? '"Come back! Come back!" yelled the little—'"

"Poppy! Stop touching me with your foot!" Lucy said, whipping her body out of the covers as if she'd been grazed by a snake.

"But I wanna touch you with my foot!" Poppy said, hurt but also entitled.

"Girls! Please! Are we reading this or not? Stop bickering and listen or I'll put the book away right now."

"No, Mommy. Please keep reading!" they said in chorus.

"All right then," I said, firm and proper like Mary Poppins. I cleared my throat. "Where was I? Oh yes, 'But the Gingerbread Man just looked over his shoulder and said, "No! No! I won't come back! I'd rather run than be your snack!"'"

"Can I please have a banana? Look at me, Mommy. I look so, so, so, so, so hungry," Lucy said, breathless, as if stranded on an island.

"Absolutely not. It's bedtime, and before bed I gave you an avocado with salt, per your request, which is plenty of food for the night. Now, can I continue, please?"

"What's that say?"

"Thirteen, Poppy! It's page thirteen!"

This went on and on, as it does every night. I try to read, they constantly interrupt, I threaten to leave, they beg me to stay.

But I always perk up when the fox appears because he eats the Gingerbread Man, which means I can finally get on with the portion of my evening that doesn't involve my kids. With pep, I said, "And quick as a wink, before he could think, the Gingerbread Man was gone."

"Did the fox kill him?" Lucy asked, disturbed, as if this ending was new and not something she had heard nightly for months.

"Yes, he ate him."

"Did it hurt?"

"No, he's a cookie."

"But he's a cookie that talks and runs like a person!" Lucy reasoned. "Why did he eat him?"

"Well . . . because he was a cookie, and he's delicious! And the Gingerbread Man was going around taunting everybody. Can you imagine? Being all delicious, taunting people to eat you, and then running away? It's just rude."

"What does *taunting* mean?" Lucy asked.

"Um. Hmm. Like, teasing, I guess. Sort of luring . . . maybe? Like taunting." I never realized what a nightmare employee I'd be if I worked at Merriam-Webster until I had girls constantly asking me what words meant. One evening, while taking her sweet time on a restaurant toilet, Lucy asked, "What does *what do you mean*, mean?" To which I replied, "What do you mean, 'what do you mean'? It means 'what do you mean'!" For a writer, you'd think I'd be more skilled, but for some reason if you ask me what a word means, I honestly have no idea.

"Does he need a ban-naid?" Poppy interjected.

"No, he doesn't feel pain. And he was gobbled up by the fox, so no need for Band-Aids, all right?" The girls sunk in, knowing that the day was almost through, trying to savor the very last seconds by conjuring up more questions before the lights went out.

I held both girls in my arms and kissed the tops of their heads. Freshly bathed, their hair smelled sweet and good and innocent. I noticed two new freckles on the swoop of Lucy's nose. Her eyelashes were so long that I was sure no child in the history of children had eyelashes as long, full, and gorgeous as hers. I looked over at Poppy, her lips always big and red like she's wearing lipstick. She's so cute it makes my heart beat fast.

It's always the simple, mundane moments, the tiniest details of my beloveds, that give me the most courage. A pandemic could be burning through like a brushfire outside our doorstep. Doom and gloom and sarcasm and meanness rolling through my newsfeed all day, every day, as it does. The world could crumble around us; my enemy could become a *New York Times* bestselling author; my best friend could lose twenty pounds. My latest essay could flop; fans could unfollow; mean comments could run amok. My favorite comfy pants could go thin at the inner thigh. I could get sick or go bankrupt, be estranged from someone I love, attend a funeral, get the flu on Christmas Day, or lose every single thing I own. Yet tucked away in our twin-size bed, with our faces glowing by dim light, I just knew, no matter what—we would be all right.

Deep in my soul, it is well.

It's kind of embarrassing when you think about it. Who needs to be liked by strangers when so loved by little girls audacious enough to ask for avocado with salt right before bed? My mind wandered to the moment years before when I cried in the bathtub, miscarriage looming, begging God to let me keep my baby. I wish I could go back and soothe her, give her a picture of this moment. I know the pain is unbearable, but it will get better. In fact, it will get so good some days I'll want to burst into tears. Would I have believed me? I think so. That's what's made faith so magical in my life—the audacity to believe God for the impossible is what brought those very things to life.

So many moments were supposed to be the beginning of the end. Apocalyptic, even. And they just . . . weren't. Continuous, rolling, anticlimactic dramas. Vanity of vanities, it's all just vanity. So much time spent worrying over things that never even happened! Worrying about things that didn't even matter.

Because, really, it may seem grim in the moment, but we'll laugh about it . . . someday. Just give it a little time.

And I know it, and I feel it, every time I read my girls a bedtime story.

"Riddle-riddle ran, fiddle-fiddle fan, so ends the story of the Gingerbread Man," I said softly at the end of our story. I closed the book, kissed their foreheads tenderly, and whispered into their ears how much I loved them.

As I left the room and slipped the book back onto the shelf, I couldn't help but feel deep within my heart—the Gingerbread Man really did have it coming.

ACKNOWLEDGMENTS

C an we give my mom, Christine Lind, a round of applause? Every writer needs a person to write to—and I've always written to my mom. She comforts me when my work's rejected, screams and dances when it's accepted. I know it's not right, but I feel deeply entitled to her time. If she doesn't return my texts within two minutes, I contact everyone in the family to hunt her down. If my efforts are fruitless, I call the cops. She is the reason I write—and write well enough to thank her in the acknowledgments of my first book. A brilliant writer in her own right, Mom reads and edits my work so I don't embarrass myself. I make her drop everything to listen to my first drafts. If she doesn't guffaw at the funny parts, I pause and say, "Why aren't you laughing?" Oh, the pressure this poor woman's been under! But when it's bad, she tells me so. And when it's good, we spend the rest of the afternoon talking about how good it is. This is my greatest joy, talking about how good my writing is for hours, with a person who delights in me so. Thank you, Mom. We have fun together, don't we?

I must thank the funniest person I know, my dad. He doted on me so relentlessly as a child that I developed a false sense of security, truly believing I was God's gift to all mankind. This gave me the courage to put my writing out into the world. I soon realized that I wasn't, in fact, God's gift to all mankind—at least according to mankind—but by then it was too late, and the writing bug stuck. You spoiled me rotten with your love, and it was the best gift you could have given me.

Thank you to my sister, Jenny, for helping to raise me—for being my best friend. We have a YouTube channel called "Jenny and Anna Bake," and it might be the best thing to ever happen to me. I love you, Buddy! And to my big, strong brother, Christian, who defended me when I was little and often forgets to bring the chips to our family gatherings—thank you for making me feel so safe.

Now, to my husband, Rob. He's not perfect, but he's close. He's held *the worst* jobs so I could write. He moves aside so I can shine. He loves my cooking and takes care of our girls' bath time. He removes spiders from my presence and carries heavy things when I'd rather not. We share a beautiful family together, and when it's good, it's real good, and when it's bad, eh—it's not too shabby. I love you, babe. Thank you.

To my beloved lifelong friends, Jen, Brady, and Amber—thank you for letting me use your real names and share our hysterical stories. My life is so funny and rich with you in my life. To Lacy, who was by my side our entire childhood, yes, I put the period story in my first book. I wish you were here to read it. I still have vivid dreams about you—and I say all the things I should have said before you died. One day I'll write about you; I just have to find the words.

Let me meander to my literary agent, Erin Niumata. Every writer deserves an agent who believes in them, fights for them, scoffs at their haters, and counsels them when they get all up in their feels. Not every writer has one, but I do with Erin. She's also hilarious and has appropriate boundaries when I've tried to become best friends. I'll wear her down eventually and soon our families will celebrate Christmas together. Thank you, Erin—I love you. (Too soon?)

And when I say my editor at Nelson Books, Jenny Baumgartner, was straight up answered prayer, I mean it. Thank you, Jenny, for giving me this incredible opportunity. You get my humor and vision; you give me free rein to be myself. You're so smart and have such a sharp eye, pulling out the very best of me. Thank you for your mentorship. If I could give you a hug, it would be one of those awkwardly long ones where you eventually pat my back and gently pull away.

Of course, Jenny wasn't alone—the entire Nelson Books team are some of the most brilliant and kindest people I've ever met. Thank you, Kristina Juodenas, for bringing the vision of my cover to life—it is perfect. To the marketing genius, Stephanie Tresner, thank you. I feel so confident in your hands. Thank you to editor Lauren Langston Stewart, for your steady guidance and shiny polish during the final stages of my book's creation. To copy editor Whitney Bak—thank you. A lot of writers don't like to be edited, but when it's done by such thoughtful, talented professionals, it's actually a lot of fun. To Sara Broun and those behind-the-scenes who worked so hard on my behalf, thank you. You have all blessed me beyond words.

To my most wonderful friend and publicist, Danelle Schlegelmilch, you're simply the best, you know that? We met at a church potluck. I complimented your Chinese chicken salad, and you told me it was just one of those prebagged salads from Costco. We've been inseparable ever since. The way you've supported my career and spent countless unpaid hours dreaming with me . . . well, it could make me weep if I thought real hard about it. From the bottom of my heart, thank you.

And lastly, I must thank my precious girls, Lucy and Poppy. *You are* God's gift to all mankind; I don't care what mankind says. You make me and your daddy so proud. As I'm writing this, you are four and six years old, sitting under my desk, playing, giggling, and occasionally fistfighting. We are so in love, us three. We'll always be best friends and have each other's backs, *you hear me*? We'll laugh and laugh, love and love, all our livelong days. Don't ever forget what I tell you at bedtime—*we are* The Thomas Girls, *and we can do anything we set our minds to.*

It's true. A whole life of adventure awaits.

NOTES

1. Dr. Ali Binazir, "Are You a Miracle? On the Probability of Your Being Born," HuffPost, updated August 16, 2011, https://www.huffpost.com/entry/probability-being-born_b_877853.
2. *Love on the Spectrum*, season 1, episode 2, released July 22, 2020, on Netflix, https://www.netflix.com/title/81265493.
3. Shannon Lee, *Be Water, My Friend: The Teachings of Bruce Lee* (New York: Flatiron Books, 2020), 1.

ABOUT THE AUTHOR

Anna Lind Thomas is a writer, humorist, and host of the *It's Not That Serious Podcast*. She also costars in the popular YouTube series "Jenny and Anna Bake." She founded the wildly successful and now retired humor site for women HaHas for HooHas, where several of her essays have gone viral, including columns written for the *Omaha World-Herald* and Disney's *Babble*. Anna lives in Omaha, Nebraska, with her husband, Rob, and their two little girls.

She'd love to hang with you on Facebook at https://Facebook.com/AnnaLindThomas or on Instagram at @anna.lind.thomas. And if you love the book, text her at 402-915-1727. It'll make her day. *Seriously.*